Social Housing in Rural Areas

Mark Bevan, Stuart Cameron, Mike Coombes, Tanya Merridew and Simon Raybould

Published for the Joseph Rowntree Foundation by the Chartered Institute of Housing

The Chartered Institute of Housing
The Chartered Institute of Housing is the professional organisation for all people who work in housing. Its purpose is to maximise the contribution that housing professionals make to the well-being of communities. The Institute has more than 17,000 members working in local authorities, housing associations, the private sector and educational Institutions.

Chartered Institute of Housing
Octavia House, Westwood Way
Coventry CV4 8JP
Telephone: 024 7685 1700

The Joseph Rowntree Foundation
The Joseph Rowntree Foundation has supported this project as part of its programme of research and innovative development projects, which it hopes will be of value to policy makers, practitioners and service users. The facts presented and views expressed in this report, however, are those of the authors and not necessarily those of the Foundation.

Joseph Rowntree Foundation
The Homestead
40 Water End
York YO30 6WP
Telephone: 01904 629241

Social housing in rural areas
Mark Bevan, Stuart Cameron, Mike Coombes, Tanya Merridew and Simon Raybould.
The Joseph Rowntree Foundation is very grateful to Cath Murphy for her skill in editing and structuring the material in this report to produce a clear, accessible account of the research undertaken by the team.

© JRF/CIH 2001

Published for the Joseph Rowntree Foundation by the Chartered Institute of Housing
ISBN 1 903208 17 3

Graphic design by Jeremy Spencer
Cover illustration by Paul Johnson with Alan Dearling
Editorial management by Alan Dearling
Printed by Hobbs the Printers, Totton

CONTENTS

TABLES AND FIGURES

ACKNOWLEDGEMENTS

We are indebted to a large number of people for helping us in the preparation of this report. We have benefited from the support of Tony Champion and others in Newcastle University's Housing & Society Research Group, as well as from numerous secretarial and other colleagues.

We would particularly like to acknowledge the help and patience of our Advisory Group: Trevor Cherrett, Sussex Rural Community Council; Margaret Clark, The Countryside Agency; Allan Findlay, Dundee University; Theresa McDonagh, The Joseph Rowntree Foundation; Fergus Murray, Penwith Housing Association; Steve Ongeri, The Housing Corporation; Mark Shucksmith, Aberdeen University; and Andrew Williamson, Hastoe Housing Association.

Last but by no means least we would like to thank those who provided the information upon which the research is based.

- Special thanks are due to the local authorities, registered social landlords and residents who gave their time to help us with the research.

- Nick Buck and colleagues in Essex University prepared and supplied data from the British Household Panel Survey: this dataset was supplied via the Data Archive.

- Brian Dodgeon at the Institute of Education in London University prepared and supplied Longitudinal Study data: this dataset is Crown Copyright and was provided courtesy of the Office for National Statistics.

- Peter Lee of Birmingham University generously made available ward-level estimates of average earnings.

EXECUTIVE SUMMARY

Much of rural England experiences problems of access to and affordability of housing. House prices have been driven up by the influx of the affluent. The already low level of provision of council housing has been diminished by generally high levels of Right to Buy sales. In recent years, registered social landlords (RSLs) – mostly housing associations – have become the main providers of new social rented housing, often using land provided by special planning mechanisms.

The aim of this research was to investigate the current role of such housing in rural areas. Interview surveys in five case study areas were used to explore the experiences of residents and housing providers. A classification of rural housing markets was developed to provide a framework for case study selection reflecting the variations in circumstances in different parts of rural England, and also as a framework for the analysis of large-scale data sets – of small area and individual longitudinal data – to attempt to identify links between housing market type, housing change and a range of demographic characteristics.

■ The experience of residents

The experience of most residents of rural social housing was very positive, and they felt that their housing needs could not have been so adequately met by other housing options available in the locality.

Beyond the value of the housing accommodation itself, the opportunity to maintain family and neighbour networks was the clearest benefit identified by those tenants with connections to the locality. However, many respondents who had come from elsewhere also identified substantial benefits from their new home and from a rural location. On the other hand, a minority who had moved from elsewhere found that their location resulted in isolation and lack of access to facilities and opportunities.

Benefits in terms of links to the local labour market were less obvious, in part because of the widespread acceptance of substantial commuting as a normal feature of employment in contemporary rural areas.

■ The experience of providers

The experience of RSLs in providing housing in rural areas reflected a number of dilemmas and problems.

While a shortage of affordable rural housing was the general context to which RSLs were responding, many shared with their urban counterparts concerns about lack of demand in specific locations and housing types. The small population base in rural areas made attempts to quantify and measure very localised 'housing need' vulnerable to fluctuations in local demand.

'Local need' conditions, restricting occupation to those with a local connection, were often attached to planning consents and incorporated into allocation criteria. This had mixed implications for rural RSLs. It was sometimes seen in a positive light, involving more sensitivity to local opinion and a move away from purely needs-based allocations – a 'community housing' approach which put rural RSLs in the forefront of national trends in allocations policies. On the other hand, RSLs commonly felt that the imposition of occupancy restrictions through Section 106 planning agreements creates undesirable inflexibility. Problems with attracting private finance and letting property could arise, and the effects could be exclusionary in ignoring wider housing needs.

RSLs in rural areas also shared 'urban' concerns about 'residualisation' and social exclusion in social housing. Partnership approaches with other agencies were seen as the way forward in addressing these issues. In many areas, though, the major contribution made by rural social housing to the creation of mixed and socially-inclusive communities was in the very fact of providing housing opportunities for those with lower income where otherwise the housing market catered only for the affluent.

■ Variations between rural housing markets

There is substantial variation in market conditions between rural areas in different parts of England. As part of the research a classification of rural housing markets was developed which differentiates housing markets on issues such as the levels of social housing provision, the loss through Right to Buy, the 'tightness' of the market conditions and the nature of housing demand. Those villages where social housing is a continuing feature tend to be rather economically depressed (former pit villages provide the most dramatic example). These areas' loss of local job opportunities proves to have more influence than the local availability of social housing on the decisions of, for example, young people to move away.

More generally, the classification of rural housing markets illustrates how issues of housing provision cannot be divorced from the wider social and economic dynamics which impact very differently in different parts of rural England.

CHAPTER 1

INTRODUCTION AND CONTEXT

Lack of affordable housing is a central issue for much of rural England (Bramley and Smart, 1995; Shucksmith *et al*, 1996). In many areas it is the result of a combination of the high cost of housing to buy, and a low level of alternative provision in the social rented sector.

The movement of higher income commuter households to rural localities has resulted in sustained rises in house prices, taking owner occupation beyond the reach of many local people (Shucksmith, 1981). In some sought after areas, prices have risen as a result of people with substantial housing equity retiring to the countryside from urban areas, and demand for holiday and second homes.

Historically, local authorities have tended to build relatively few houses for rent in rural areas (Phillips and Williams, 1982), and this pattern has been repeated in housing association development (Chaplin *et al*, 1995). More recently, the stock of publicly owned dwellings in many rural areas has been substantially reduced through the Right to Buy (RTB) scheme (Forrest and Murie, 1992), with council stock almost disappearing in some areas. At the same time, new development by local authorities had almost halted, so council houses bought under the scheme have not been replaced.

Towards the end of the 1980s there was a growing recognition of the need to address the shortfall of new affordable dwellings in rural areas. Bramley (1990) identified an 'affordability gap' between local house prices and local incomes, particularly in rural areas in the south of England, which increased awareness of the problem. In response, greater use was made of the planning system to encourage the provision of new affordable housing (notably through 'exceptions sites'), and new funding mechanisms were introduced, such as the Housing Corporation's Rural Programme and supplementary credit approval to rural local authorities. The new housing that has resulted includes low-cost home ownership, shared ownership and privately rented accommodation managed by housing associations as well as social rented accommodation. The Rural White Paper, published in November 2000, sets out new proposals for affordable housing and these are summarised in Appendix 1.

The focus of this research is social rented housing provided by RSLs in rural areas. There are two strands to the investigation – a quantitative analysis for England as a whole using the 1991 Census and longitudinal study data, and qualitative material from users and providers of social housing in five case study areas.

❑ Rural housing and social exclusion

A related issue concerns the relationships between residents of new social rented housing and other members of those rural communities. As suggested above, one objective of social rented housing in rural areas might be to help sustain communities by providing low-income residents with an opportunity to remain within that locality. At the same time, the opposition to housing association developments from some members of rural communities, and the stigma sometimes faced by households who live in such developments, has been highlighted by research (Simmons, 1997). In part, opposition to a housing development may be based upon concern over new development in a village *per se*, but it may also be connected to the kinds of perceptions and prejudices which lead the tenants of some social housing developments to face social exclusion.

Recent policy debate has linked issues of rural social housing provision and need with broader social and environment issues and objectives within the countryside. The paper on *Rural Economies* produced by the Policy and Innovation Unit, as part of the consultation process for the Rural White Paper, suggests that,

> *"...without adequate provision of social and affordable housing, large parts of rural England risk becoming the near-exclusive preserve of the more affluent sections of society. This risk poses an important challenge to the goal of achieving balanced communities."*

(Performance and Innovation Unit, 1999, para 1.36)

In 1999, the Department for the Environment, Transport and the Regions (DETR) and the Ministry of Agriculture, Fisheries and Food (MAFF) issued a discussion document, *Rural England*, identifying *"a fair and inclusive society"* as one of the government's objectives for rural areas. Many responses to the paper linked this objective to the issue of housing. For example, the representations by the Joseph Rowntree Foundation suggested that,

> *"…a considerable body of research reveals a widespread and severe shortage of low-cost housing in rural areas which is recognised as not only a major contributor to rural disadvantage but also as the principal engine of social change in rural England. This is particularly important in excluding indigenous younger households on low incomes, unable to own their own property and with limited opportunities available in the rental market."*
> (Joseph Rowntree Foundation, 1999, p. 6)

❑ Local need

Housing providers have a number of reasons for developing social housing in rural areas. These include:

- most commonly, to address local housing needs, in particular the impact on low-income households, especially young people, of the high cost of buying housing;

- to help sustain rural communities, where numbers of full-time residents are dropping due to pressure on prices through demand for second and holiday homes;

- to help maintain social networks between generations of families who live and work in the countryside;

- to support the continuity of facilities and services in rural areas by sustaining the numbers of full-time residents working in the area.

In rural areas, new social housing provision by registered social landlords[1] (RSLs) is influenced by three main factors:

- Identification and analysis of local housing need, which is an essential element in justifying the development, both its inclusion within the

---

1   The term registered social landlord is used to encompass traditional housing associations and new forms of non-profit making organisations, such as local housing companies, in keeping with the usage introduced in the 1996 Housing Act. In fact all the RSLs included in the report are housing associations.

funded development programme of an RSL and the release of land with planning permission. This is especially the case where this involves the allocation of land as an 'exception' to existing residential land allocations.

- Planning obligations, which are often attached to the initial planning permission – using Section 106 of the Town and Country Planning Act – stipulating that all residents must have at least family or work connections to the local area.

- In the case of social rented housing 'local connection' may also be used, as an allocation criterion – RSLs most often require tenants to have a local connection in schemes where there is a planning obligation, or some other agreement or condition attached to the development.

The concept of 'local need' is central to much rural social housing provision, but the meaning of both 'local' and 'need' raise important questions. Within rural housing policy, 'local' is often applied at the level of a specific village or parish, rather than district level. This reflects the understanding of the term by many rural residents and of most applicants for rural social housing, who will often only seek housing within a specific village or small town. Meeting the objective of maintaining rural social networks, for example, often depends on a very localised approach, but it can lead to inflexibility and difficulties in accurately matching and maintaining a balance between supply and demand. Wider patterns of housing need (for example, homeless households from other nearby localities) may also need to be taken into account, otherwise there is a danger that higher levels of needs in nearby areas are unmet, or the 'local need' criterion is used as an exclusionary device to prevent people in the wider area from being housed within a locality where they might be seen to be 'undesirable' neighbours.

❏ A rural dimension to 'urban' policy issues

There are a number of key policy issues relating to housing and social inclusion which are usually discussed in an urban context, but which also have a rural dimension.

■ Residualisation and low demand

Residualisation is a major issue in the future role of social housing in England. Lee and Murie (1997) argue that this phenomenon is due not only to changes in the social, economic and demographic characteristics of the sector, but also to public perceptions of social housing as 'stigmatised'.

If this is so, social housing may be increasingly occupied by reluctant residents, creating the low-demand and high turnover, which can result in neighbourhood break down (Power and Mumford, 1999; Richardson and Corbishley, 1999). However, demand for social housing varies widely across the country, with urban areas in northern Britain being more affected by low-demand than the south-east and rural areas across the country (DTZ Pieda Consulting, 1998). Even so many of the conditions and problems which give rise to low demand in urban settings can be found in rural England – former coalfield communities represent the most obvious example. Even in rural areas less affected by employment and population loss, more specific and localised problems of demand can arise in parts of the social housing stock.

In the past, council housing was, like owner occupation, seen as one possible 'destination tenure' of a housing career; in contrast, the private rented sector tended to play a more temporary role as a 'stepping stone' to a more permanent tenure. The long-term growth of home ownership may now have led to social housing too being seen by many not as a destination but as a stepping stone, with the result that demand is now more temporary and transitory. The implications affect RSLs in rural as well as urban areas. Forrest and Murie (1992) conclude that rural housing providers may be especially vulnerable to the impact of a future in which demand is more transitory, and turnover higher, because the small scale of development in rural areas increases the difficulty of matching supply to a localised and unstable pattern of demand.

■ Forms of exclusion in housing

An important distinction must be made between exclusion from housing and exclusion *through* housing (Marsh and Mullins, 1998). In the large, low-demand, council estates, it is exclusion through housing which is most obvious: housing is readily available, but may bring with it exclusionary problems of stigma, lack of opportunity, and high levels of crime and harassment. By contrast, exclusion *from* housing – lack of access to affordable housing – is the most obvious problem in many rural areas. Nevertheless, even where social housing is available in a rural setting it may bring its own exclusion *through* housing in the form of the stigma and isolation of not being part of the owner occupying majority.

Wider issues, such as the need for access to employment, services, transport and social networks must also be considered in developing and allocating social housing in the countryside. For example, the Chartered Institute of Housing (1999, p. 5) notes that,

> "...in addressing the housing problems in rural areas it is important that wider sustainability issues are also addressed to make rural living viable for those on lower incomes. If there is insufficient access to jobs, health care, public transport etc. then demand for housing from local people, particularly young adults, is likely to ebb away."

The same paper also reports the finding of research carried out by Warwick District Council that,

> "...for poor people living there [i.e. the rural areas of the District] the relative wealth of many people living in the countryside made them feel uncomfortable because the differences in lifestyle between rich and poor were more apparent." (ibid, p. 6)

Housing providers that are aware that social housing provision does not in itself solve all the problems of social exclusion facing low-income residents of rural areas have played a wider role in supporting their tenants through a 'Housing Plus' role in rural areas (Oldfield King Planning, 1997).

■ Mixed communities

The promotion of more socially mixed communities is a common theme of much recent debate and policy (Jupp, 2000). In practice, the challenge of developing balanced communities in many rural localities is the exact reverse of that in large urban council estates. In the latter the emphasis is on breaking up large social housing developments, largely through promoting owner occupation. In rural areas the maintenance of balanced communities depends on *expanding* the social rented sector.

❏ Aims and methods of the research

The overall aim of this research is to examine the impact of recent social housing in rural areas. Issues of housing need will be considered alongside access to employment, social networks and local services in rural locations. In order to do this, three sources of information were used:

- A ward-level classification of rural housing markets was developed (discussed in Chapter 2). This provided data for each housing market type on issues including settlement type, location, housing, employment and migration. It was also used for the selection of five case study areas for detailed interview-based study.

- Interviews in the five case study areas of RSLs and their tenants, focussing on residents' perspectives on the role social housing plays for them and the policies, practices and experience of agencies involved in the delivery and management of social housing in rural areas.

- An analysis of longitudinal data from the Longitudinal Study and the British Household Panel Survey (described in Appendix 5), which provided data on housing, employment and migration careers and health and well-being.

The next chapter explains how the case study areas for the quantitative analysis were selected and gives some background data on each. Chapter 3 examines how rural social housing meets the needs of local housing, Chapter 4 looks at the relationship between housing and other issues such as employment in rural areas. Chapter 5 looks at the experience of those agencies providing housing in rural areas and Chapter 6 gives the conclusions that can be drawn from the analysis of the material.

CHAPTER 2

CLASSIFICATION OF RURAL HOUSING MARKETS

The classification used to select the five case study areas is a derivative of the rural housing markets typology, jointly produced for the Department of the Environment (DoE) by Aberdeen and Newcastle Universities (Shucksmith *et al*, 1995). The DoE study emphasised that a single typology could only represent a minority of the many aspects to rural housing markets and as well as the specific classification defined from the DoE's use, details were given of several statistical axes underlying that classification so that different typologies could be identified for different research needs. This study takes forward that approach, adapting and updating the DoE classification to meet present needs.

❑ England's changing housing markets

There were six core elements of the DoE classification. It was:

- restricted to England
- based on 1981 wards
- restricted to rural areas from the outset
- structured by three axes devised on *a priori* grounds
- calibrated primarily with 1981 Census data
- updated partially with 1991 Census data.

For the present research, a classification based on 1991 wards is used, which then allows these areas to be linked with the postcode-based data in the British Household Panel Survey and the longitudinal research reported later. However, adopting 1991 wards as the 'building blocks' for the classification meant that substantial technical obstacles had to be overcome.

❑ Definition of rural areas

There are many ways to define what constitutes a rural area and the classification used here is that of the Countryside Agency which follows the former Rural Development Commission's approach of deeming *all* areas to be rural except for settlements of 10,000 people or more (Countryside Agency, 1999) operating at the detailed sub-ward level of Enumeration Districts. Settlements are here taken to be continuous built-up areas, from the DoE (1993) definition. Thus wards are defined as 'rural' if the majority of their population live in Enumeration Districts that are *not* part of settlements with a 1991 population of 10,000 or more.

A substantial number of smaller towns lie within this definition of rural areas, because urban settlements with 1991 populations below the 10,000 threshhold are included and some of these small urban settlements include more than one 1991 ward. It is not realistic to analyse two wards in the same small town as if they were separate housing markets, so the solution here has been to group together wards whose residents mostly live in the same town. As a result, the 'rural areas' described below are either individual wards – most of which cover a single village or a group of small villages – or are groups of wards which each approximate to a single small town. Appendix 2 compares this set of rural areas with the localities identified in the Housing Corporation and Rural Development Commission's Rural Settlement Gazetteer (Bibby and Shepherd, 1997). Any definition of urban and rural areas reflects just one out of numerous different alternative approaches, as shown by the fact that some of the 'urban' settlements in the DoE (1993) definitions have populations which are low enough for them to be eligible for Housing Corporation assistance for settlements with fewer than 3,000 residents.

❑ Classification method

There is a wide variety in rural housing markets which must be reflected in this analysis. Therefore, after the urban wards were removed from the database, factor analyses were used to classify and group the different types of rural areas. The three axes on which this classification was based were:

- Axis 1 – emphasises the difference between areas in housing land supply constraints, differentiating areas of tight supply and those where supply is less constrained.

- Axis 2 – provides an overview of the source of housing demand in each area distinguishing especially areas dominated by out-commuting from those under pressure from holidaymakers or in-migrants of retirement age.
- Axis 3 – looks at the original level of social housing within the area and, where this was comparatively high, the extent to which it has been reduced by Right to Buy sales.

This analysis produced 6 classes of rural housing markets. Appendix 3 shows the way in which the classification was developed and some of the technical barriers that had to be overcome.

❏ Six classes of rural housing markets

From this analysis, six classes of rural markets can be identified. Classes 1 and 2 have at least 20 per cent of their 1981 housing stock as social housing. This is a high proportion and similar to that found in urban areas. Areas in class 1 had retained at least this proportion through to 1991 whereas those in class 2 had experienced a decline in this proportion by at least 7.5 percentage points over the 1980s. As a basis for comparison, Denham and White (1998) reported in 1991 that just over 10 per cent of housing in rural England as a whole was publicly rented.

The class 1 areas include several concentrations in parts of the country associated with coal mining, most notably in the north-east and either side of the Yorkshire/Nottinghamshire border, but also in some small former coalfields such as the Forest of Dean. The other main concentration of class 1 areas is in northern Fenland where the local agriculture developed to a virtually industrial scale. A looser scatter of class 1 areas stretches from Dorset to Norfolk (including some military bases in Wiltshire and East Anglia), but more of the areas in this part of the country are class 2.

Class 2 areas also have had a high proportion of social housing but this has declined as a result of policies such as RTB. These areas are mainly in southern England, extending to parts of the midlands and north of England, but in these regions class 1 is more prevalent in all but scenic or 'deep rural' countryside such as Herefordshire and the Pennine dales.

Classes 3 and 4 are areas where social housing has not been a very significant factor, but those where the pressures on the local housing stock are fuelled by in-migrants who are predominantly in the family-building age groups, and where out-commuting from the immediate area is important. Unsurprisingly these areas are most commonly found near to the largest urban areas. The areas are then separated into classes 3 and 4 according to the 'tightness' of their housing supply.

The class 3 areas have severe housing supply constraints and are mainly southern, primarily within commuting range of London or Bristol (or, in a few cases, Manchester). In fact there are so many class 3 areas circling the capital that they would probably form a 'doughnut' around London were it not for the numerous urban areas closely spaced throughout the Home Counties region.

Class 4 areas have lower supply-side constraints and all lie to the north of an arc from Wiltshire via the Chilterns to the Suffolk coast. Class 4 embraces many areas conveniently located for commuting to one or more of the midland and northern cities ranging from Birmingham to Hull (or, to a lesser extent, Teesside or Tyneside).

Classes 5 and 6 are the areas where recent in-migrants have included a substantial proportion of people of retirement age, or there is a significant presence of second homes and holiday accommodation. Again these are separated into groups according to the level of constraints on the supply side of their housing markets, giving a largely south-north split between classes 5 and 6 respectively. The picture is not quite so clear-cut in this case because constraints on new house building in the northern national parks places a substantial constraint on housing supply in many villages here (Wong and Madden, 2000), placing them in class 5. To some extent, class 6 is a 'residual' category covering those villages without any of the defining characteristics qualifying them for the other classes.

❏ How do the classes compare?

Table 1 examines the size of rural settlements associated with each class (no settlement can have over 10,000 residents according to the definition of 'rural' used here). Few residents of either class 5 or class 6 (high proportion of retirees and second homes) live in large villages or small towns of over 3,000 people. At the other end of the spectrum, class 1 (continued high social

Table 1: Percent of population in settlements of at least 3,000 people

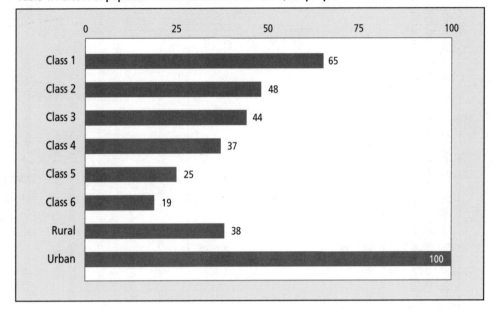

housing) is closest to being 'urban countryside' because nearly two out of every three residents live in large villages or small towns.

Tables 2 and 3 summarise some of the differences between areas in each of the housing market classes:

- Class 1 (sustained high social housing) has much of its population in small towns, whereas the large majority of class 6 and class 5 residents live in smaller settlements.

- Class 1 areas differ from other rural areas by showing several rather urban attributes, and in particular have a high male unemployment rate and low incomes.

- Class 1, and even more so class 4 and class 6 areas (low constraint on new building), are almost exclusively to be found in the north and midlands whilst the others are more numerous in the south, especially class 3, where there is high housing demand from families and commuters and tight constraint on new build.

- Class 6 and class 5 areas, where housing pressure is from 'retirees' and second/holiday homes, are mostly remote from larger cities.

- Class 4 and especially class 3 include substantial numbers of relatively prosperous 'commuter villages'.

Table 2: Key contrasts between classes of rural areas

For each variable, the area's value is shown as a % of the England average	Share of 1990-1 in-migrants that are of pensionable age	Share of 1991 housing that is holiday or second homes	Estimated mix-weighted average 1998-9 house price	1991 rate of owner occupancy by average earners	1991 rate of male unemployment	Average income (estimated from local occupations)
Class 1 [Trimdon]	118	93	91	98	90	94
Class 2 [Winslow]	128	136	102	102	61	103
Class 3 [Lingfield]	84	69	118	105	50	111
Class 4 [Haworth]	111	50	87	111	48	108
Class 5 [Lynton]	176	510	106	103	69	103
Class 6 [Spilsby]	178	292	89	109	68	103
All rural areas	127	170	99	104	64	104
All urban areas	97	92	100	100	104	98

Notes:
In order to assist in interpreting this and Table 3, for each of the housing market classes an 'exemplar' village has been identified (in all cases, **not** in any of the case study areas). They are:
- Trimdon in County Durham, the Prime Minister's home base, is the class 1 exemplar (high social housing maintained until 1991);
- the large village of Winslow in north Buckinghamshire has been selected as the class 2 exemplar (high social housing which declined between 1981 and 1991);
- the exemplar for class 3 (low social housing, housing pressure from families and commuters, tight constraint on new building) is Lingfield, near London, one of many villages within commuting distance of the capital;
- the exemplar for class 4 (low social housing, pressure from families, but lower constraint on new build) is Haworth, near Bradford (the Brontë village);
- the north Devon coastal village of Lynton is the exemplar village of class 5 (low social housing, pressure from 'retirees' and second homes, tight constraint on new building); and
- the tiny Lincolnshire market town of Spilsby is the class 6 exemplar (low social housing, pressure from 'retirees' and second homes, lower constraint on new building).

Table 3: Summary of rural housing market classes' distinctive characteristics

Class	1	2	3	4	5	6
exemplar	*Trimdon*	*Winslow*	*Lingfield*	*Haworth*	*Lynton*	*Spilsby*
Defining features						
Axis 3: social housing	still substantial	much 1980s RTB	not substantial	not substantial	not substantial	not substantial
Axis 2: 'typical' in-migrant	mixed	mixed	out-commuter	out-commuter	retiree/second homes	retiree/second homes
Axis 1: housing market	mixed	mixed	very 'tight'	less constrained	constrained	less constrained
Regional location	more in north	more in south	south	north	south (or national park)	north
Sub-regional	some coalfields	mixed	home counties	near big cities	more peripheral	more peripheral
Settlement size	mostly larger	some larger	mixed	mixed	few larger	few larger
Other economic state	struggling	mixed	prospering	prospering	mixed	mixed
Overview 'stereotype'	more 'urban' countryside	where RTB was dominant	'stockbroker belt' villages	prosperous commuter villages	coast/country attracting holidaymakers	more 'ordinary' countryside

These factors can have a bearing on the analysis of the different classes of rural housing markets in the following chapters and this will be taken into account. For example, differences between class 1 and the other housing market classes may, on the one hand, be due to class 1's higher level of social housing provision in 1991 or, on the other, be reflecting the relatively high level of poverty and unemployment in those same areas.

❏ Selection of case study areas for the interview survey

Using the housing market classification as a framework, five case study areas, each comprising a local authority district, were selected within which interviews were carried out with providers and tenants of recently-constructed social rented RSL housing, as well as with representatives of local authorities and parish councils.

The case studies were drawn from different regions of England and each case study was, as far as possible, representative of one class within the ward-level classification of rural housing market types, though inevitably there was some variation within each local authority district. Class 1 (high social renting) was represented by a district in north-west England, class 2 (reduced social renting) by a distict in the east midlands; class 3 (high pressure, commuting) was in the south-east, and class 5 (high pressure, retirement/holiday) in the south-west. For the purposes of the survey classes 4 and 6 (lower pressure rural areas) were combined and represented by a district in Yorkshire and Humberside.

The case study areas (summarised in Appendix 4) were selected from local authorities who had two or three RSLs with schemes funded under the Housing Corporation's Rural Programme. Areas were selected which gave a variety of RSLs – those with very large stocks, those operating at national, regional and district levels and specialist rural RSLs. The selection also made sure that villages of different sizes were covered, from very small settlements to those with populations of just under 3,000 and a variety of services and facilities available.

CHAPTER 3

MEETING A LOCAL NEED

This chapter looks at the role of social housing in meeting rural housing needs, both from the point of view of the providers of rural housing and that of the occupiers, using material from the interviews held in the five case study areas throughout England. Residents were contacted by a variety of methods. In some cases the RSL made contact, in others the researchers made contact direct. At the end of each interview, residents were asked if there were any other residents they knew who might be willing to be interviewed. Interviewees were selected to give a range of circumstances – those working, in receipt of benefit, with or without children, single parents and of different ages.

❏ Assessing housing needs

Accurate assessment of housing needs has been an important theme of national debate, especially with the current emphasis upon risk assessment, but precise identification and prediction of very localised need is problematic.

"Housing needs work, when done properly, can be a key strategic tool – where done badly it can be disastrous."
(Local authority officer, Yorkshire)

The issue of scale is crucial. Fluctuating demand amongst a small population base, where identified need translates into one or two households, means that need may evaporate overnight if these decide upon an alternative housing solution. This is especially problematic given the long lead-in times for new developments. Additionally, the hidden nature of rural need was emphasised by one RSL in the south-east who claimed that it often only became apparent after 'a lot of dredging' – and even then often not until the scheme was on the ground. RSLs are thus faced with attempting to manage unpredictability when dealing with very small numbers.

Whilst efforts have been made to develop good practice in needs analysis, the case studies reveal that a lack of trust between different agencies over the source and quality of information can be a problem. In Yorkshire, for example, there has been resentment from RSLs who feel mistakes in assessing need by the local authority have left them with costly and difficult schemes. The Rural Housing Trust in the south-east also claimed that there was 'no longer any trust' between some of the key players. Hence, although partnership working was regarded as essential to the future of rural social housing, there are some significant barriers to achieving this in practice.

Nearly all of the RSLs in the study expressed a cautious approach to any new development; commonly citing the need for holistic approaches to understanding and assessing need. Projecting future demand rather than simply identify existing demand was critical, since the specific households identified initially will not in many cases be those that are eventually housed. Many were adopting a two-stage process to assessing need, moving from an initial general assessment to a more detailed picture. Pragmatism was also an important tool – in the south-east study one officer claimed a 'good rule of thumb' was to divide the established need by half and work to that figure. In the north-west, one officer reported there was 'no real rationale' as to where and how much social housing had been developed. In the east midlands, one RSL emphasised the problem that housing demand was 'a constantly moving target'. In another example from the south-west, the local authority has rejected survey work as too blunt a tool and opted instead for a comprehensive strategy to guide action.

More recent approaches to selecting potential sites for future development may involve collecting information on rural service provision as a means of assessing village vitality. Thus community audits or village appraisals are an important part of assessing rural housing need. However, such an approach may further compound problems of rural decline in some places if RSLs adopt a 'tick list' approach and only select village locations on the basis of 'backing winners', thereby ignoring the potential role of social housing in helping to rejuvenate village services. Hence, important questions arise over the relationship between social housing provision and sustaining rural communities:

"…one of our first developments took place when the local school was actually closed – but then a vigorous campaign led by one of our tenants led to the school eventually re-opening. That just shows the importance of not just looking at the situation now, but looking at the future."
(RSL, south-west)

The majority of interviews identified the critical gate-keeping role of parish councils in the provision of rural social housing. In many cases an active parish council was seen to be the pivotal link between assessments of housing need, scheme development and gaining the support of the local planning committee. For example, one parish council in the south-east had been instrumental in securing an affordable housing development, despite a ten-year struggle to overcome a series of barriers. However, one RSL noted the case of a parish council, which was seen as difficult to work with because of its representation of landed interests:

"…we tend to work mostly in areas where there is an active parish council who invite us in. There are some villages we won't work in mainly because of a lack of suitable land and the parish council attitude. If the parish council is unreceptive then it's difficult since they are often…made up of landowners and have a key influence over land availability."

Overall, an ongoing dialogue and effective relationship with the parish council was thought essential; as one RSL in the south-east commented *"…we've never wanted to confront them."* A notable contrast was an RSL in Yorkshire who claimed:

"…we now just by-pass the parish council, they think you're working for them…we don't have an obligation to consult them and we don't do it because it's such a massive task."

Hence, although working jointly with parish councils is increasingly seen as pivotal in the supply of rural social housing, there are some places where there are significant gaps in the dialogue.

❑ Reasons for living in social housing

Another way of identifying levels of local housing need is to investigate the reasons that people had for choosing this housing type. From the point of view of those living in social housing, the main reason cited for their housing choice was the limited opportunities for them to obtain accommodation in the owner occupied sector. This was particularly acute in the south-east case study. An additional barrier was the ability to maintain mortgage repayments over a number of years, particularly relevant where respondents had insecure employment. A number of these respondents, particularly in the south-west case study area, had personal experience of losing their home through repossession after having moved to the area and bought properties.

Respondents often saw the private rented sector as an unsatisfactory long-term solution to their housing needs and emphasised its insecurity. Those who had previously rented privately focussed their concern on the type of rental agreements they had had with their landlords. Where formal arrangements existed, most commented on the short-term nature of these agreements. Others talked about situations where they had been renting from friends or members of their family. They often only had a verbal agreement, and where these tenancies had broken down, the landlord had required the respondents to leave, sometimes with very little notice.

Many respondents identified the cost of renting privately as prohibitive, particularly the need to find money to pay for deposits and difficulties in trying to reclaim the deposit subsequently. Other residents emphasised the condition of some privately rented stock, or the lack of available properties for private rent. Another factor that made respondents wary of the private rented sector was the behaviour of some landlords, particularly in relation to undertaking repairs.

Some respondents felt that, as single people or couples, they stood little chance of obtaining housing on the local authority waiting list. In this respect, RSLs were seen as providing alternative opportunities to obtain accommodation, perhaps from their use of local connection clauses that short circuited waiting lists. However, in other cases local connection clauses used by local authorities limited access by people living outside that district. One respondent had obtained a new job in a different local authority area and wanted to move nearer to her place of work, but the local authority refused an application for accommodation in their district and the respondent was forced to give up her job because of the distance she had to commute each day.

Some 'need' may only become apparent when a new housing development creates real opportunities to obtain social housing. This was reflected in the way that a number of respondents put themselves forward for new housing association accommodation. Often they were not on any waiting lists, but they had reacted to hearing that such property might be available. In a number of instances, respondents saw that a property had been vacated in their village and had rung up to enquire about rehousing. In other instances, this opportunistic approach was initiated by a friend or relative living in the village:

"…my sister, she told me about these houses going up. We saw them going up sort of thing. And then, you know, like the council meetings and all that lot, as they were going up. And you used to see them progressing. And I must of been one of the last to put my name down on the list. And that's how I heard..was my sister 'cos she was living in [village] at the time anyway. My parents live here. We all live here. It's pretty sad really. And I thought, yeah, I'm gonna do that. I'm going to try."
(Lone parent, east midlands)

❑ The role of local connections

New affordable housing in rural areas is often developed on the premise that it should be used to help meet local housing needs. When respondents were asked why they wanted to live in their current homes, many of them cited strong ties with a particular village or locality as an important reason for wanting housing association accommodation. However, there were a variety of reasons why respondents saw a local connection as important.

Many respondents suggested that the schemes provided an opportunity for them to remain within a particular village where they had lived for some time. In some respects there was a feeling that there was an element of luck that the schemes were built just as their need for accommodation became apparent. There were instances where new housing association developments had played a key role in enabling extended family networks to remain living within, or to move back to, a particular village. In three of the case studies there were instances of half the properties in small scale village developments (three out of six) being allocated to members of one local extended family. The level of satisfaction with obtaining a home in a community where strong ties existed was epitomised by one respondent:

"I thought, you know, I'm not going to get one of these, not in a million years. And, I can remember where I was at the time, as well. Phoned up and my sister actually said, she said 'I've had a letter today, we've got a house'.

Oh, congratulations and all the rest of it, you know, and it turned out I'd got one too. And she actually lives next door…so it was absolutely out of this world, yeah. I never want to move. I never want to move again. This is what I've always wanted. This is what I've always dreamt of. Just me and the kids have got this lovely big house."
(Lone parent, south-east)

Constable (1999) highlights the important role that kinship networks can play in providing support for households. This was illustrated by a number of lone parents in our study who emphasised the importance of social networks in contributing to their ability to take up work opportunities. For example, one respondent noted that being able to live in the village she grew up in meant that a trusted family friend could look after her child, reducing the cost of childcare whilst she went to work.

For a number of respondents their home offered the chance of a fresh start in life, for example, after a relationship breakdown. A new development provided an opportunity for these households to move back to a village where they had social ties. One respondent noted that being able to move into housing association accommodation had enabled her to have a base to start again, with the emotional and practical support of her parents who lived a few doors down:

"…the main consideration for moving back to [village] was having my family around me. My Mum and Dad live in the village. My Gran lives in the village and my sister lives two miles away. So when my marriage broke up it was just a case of moving back to my family, so they…I mean they help me because when I go to work they look after my children."
(Lone parent, Yorkshire)

Whilst some respondents focussed on practical reasons, others were more reflective about wanting to live in a particular location:

"I think if you have to really, really try to find an answer, you're coming down to roots. Something deep inside of your self, that says, that is where my spirit, my soul, my being wants to be. No matter what happens, that is home."
(Couple with dependent children, east midlands)

Some respondents stressed that they were used to living in a rural environment, and, given the choice, would prefer to live in the countryside compared with living in a town or city. Others wanted a rural lifestyle for their children. In particular, the majority of households with children identified the quality of the education in a village school as an important reason for living in the countryside.

However, this was not a universal view amongst those with a local connection. One respondent noted that whilst they had a local connection enabling them to obtain accommodation in a particular rural locality, they felt that this factor was an incidental reason for them. First and foremost, they needed somewhere to live, and having a local connection to an area provided the necessary priority within the allocation system to meet that need.

Many respondents emphasised that RSLs provided a more stable and secure form of housing for households who were keen to stay in the area and had been making do with other accommodation in the locality. These respondents had mainly been living in privately rented accommodation, including winter lets, and the housing was unsatisfactory for a number of reasons:

> "I was living in [village] with the girls at the time in a rented accommodation. It was full of damp and mould and everything like that. Not suitable at all."
> (Family, south-east)

In other cases the quality of the new properties presented advantages over existing social housing. For example, one respondent compared her current home with the poor quality of her previous council house in the village:

> "...it was just like you was getting nowhere. You'd try and make it look something, and you'd got damp coming in somewhere. You'd got this urine stench come in the summer – it was just in the floorboards. It was just disgusting. It was no matter how much you tried to clean it, it never got clean. But that's life. Sometimes you have the bad, sometimes you've got the good. Now I've got the good. I was over the moon when I got this place."
> (Lone parent, east midlands)

However, the development of new housing association units alongside older social housing stock could lead to tension between residents. One respondent highlighted that there had been some bad feeling between new residents who had moved into a village and established social housing residents living in older properties. This respondent stated that disputes had resulted from some of the residents in the older stock feeling that they should have been offered the chance to move to the new property ahead of incoming residents.

More mixed views were evident from those respondents without a strong local connection. Mullins (1993) suggested that people with strong ties to the settlement in which they lived were less inclined to be dissatisfied compared with those people who were rehoused in areas where they did not have social links or support networks. Some respondents in our study who had very little previous connection to the settlement where they currently lived were positive about their move; they had wanted a fresh start in a new location. A key feature of these respondents' views was the chance to move away from poor housing situations, or neighbourhoods with a poor reputation, and they often commented on the peace and quiet of their present circumstances. The actual location was not so crucial for such households:

> "...when we moved here it wasn't particularly being somewhere rural but it was about the type of house and the type of neighbourhood. They were the key things. This development was a very lucky break for us."
> (Couple, south-west)

Thus, social housing in rural areas was also playing a more strategic role in meeting broader housing need within the district. Not all schemes had a local lettings policy and some respondents were offered homes as a priority from the waiting list.

It was clear that most respondents had been very happy in achieving a positive outcome to their immediate housing needs at the time that they moved in to their new home. However, some newcomers had altered their views over time. After the initial elation of moving to a new home, a small number of respondents expressed negative views about where they lived:

> "...the initial moving in, right, and being really excited to have this brand new house, I really feel quite disillusioned and quite trapped now, living in this village. Because, and I talked to people, 'cos I couldn't really put it into words... Everybody else who lives in these new houses lived here before in the old houses. I was talking to my friend 'cos she feels the same way...It's to do with being classified. For the first time ever, I feel classified by where I live. When I've lived in rented accommodation before, you've lived in a street: nobody knows if you own the house, or even if they know you privately rent it, you're not judged by the road that you live in. And I feel very conscious of that here."
> (Couple with dependent children, south-east)

Another respondent regretted moving to a village:

> "…*if somebody wanted to live here they've really got to want to live the rural life, really, and really understand the rural life, 'cos we didn't. We were idealistic.*"
> (Couple with dependent children, Yorkshire)

Such responses illustrate that a rural lifestyle can be problematic for some, regardless of the housing.

❑ The need for flexibility

Recent research has highlighted the difficulty that residents in social housing may experience if they want to move tenure within rural localities, particularly those typified by a constrained housing market (DTZ Pieda Consulting, 1998). This places an emphasis on transfers within the social housing stock as an essential way to help households move. Indeed, a number of residents viewed their options to move home only in terms of a transfer or mutual exchange. However, one issue to emerge from the resident interviews was a conflict between local connection clauses in S106 agreements and mutual exchanges. A couple of residents stated that they would like to exercise the right to a mutual exchange, but could not find any suitable reciprocal household fitting the criteria for local connection. In this respect they felt trapped by the S106 agreement:

> "…*if we wanted to move to Surrey, we'd need to find someone in Surrey with a connection with this village. You're never going to do that. No-one's bloody heard of [village] in Surrey.*"
> (Couple with dependent child, south-east)

In a small number of cases, the lack of choice with tenancy offers was quite a significant issue for respondents. Lack of choice over location can increase the likelihood of residents moving into homes where they soon feel trapped and isolated:

> "…*I think we'd be in a no-win situation. You know, we're almost, we're resigned in ourselves that once you're here, you're pretty much stuck here. Unless you want to give up the house and just go…be all right if you won the lottery, but if you got out of here you'd probably give it up and start off again.*"
> (Couple with dependent children, south-east)

A number of RSLs also commented on the tension that exists between the statutory right to mutual exchange and the S106 agreement. One RSL, wary of increased numbers of voids, had deliberately refrained from raising awareness amongst tenants of the transfer system despite recognising the potentially divisive nature of this stance. Overall, there was a sense that more flexible local lettings requirements could contribute to a more vibrant social housing sector, and that inflexibility within the system may simply result in people leaving their tenancies.

In many rural areas, the use of a local lettings policy raises some important ethical issues relating to equal opportunities and social inclusion, though recently it has gained some support with the growing view that general needs lettings may have exacerbated social exclusion. Local connection requirements may also pose serious problems for social landlords in restricting the pool of potential tenants. Given the falling demand in some rural locations, several RSLs stressed the need for an agreed strategy from the outset about how to respond when local needs don't result in a letting.

Many RSLs have established effective cascade systems. For example, one RSL in Yorkshire had introduced a cascade beginning with parish, followed by neighbouring villages and finally district. However, in some cases it was felt that the local authority or parish council doggedly pursued local connections clauses, and that a failure to take a broader view was felt to be unhelpful.

> *"Where we have bought the land from the district council...they place even more restrictions on the development than even the parish council. They say 'you can't house so and so there because they haven't lived here for five years'. But five years is an arbitrary figure...we were not allowed to rehouse someone who owned a garage in the same village. As a consequence he moved away – shutting the garage and making two people in that village unemployed."*
> (RSL, south-west)

The inflexibility of waiting lists and allocations restricted to a single village might also be reduced through the use of village clustering. Increasingly applicants are being asked to specify areas of choice rather than single villages. In one locality, the local authority was working with the parish councils to identify the most inter-linked, rather than spatially closest, villages. This approach was seen as one way to increase flexibility within the allocation system, allowing applicants more chance of being identified for schemes that are within the vicinity of their desired location. It also perhaps reflects a growing need to work across spatial boundaries in the delivery of rural social housing, which was exemplified in the east midlands case study and is highlighted in PPG 3 (Department of Environment, Transport and the Regions, 2000).

❏ Current experiences of home

Quantitative studies have found high levels of resident satisfaction with their housing association homes in rural areas (Mullins, 1993; Oldfield King, 1997). Respondents in this study tended to echo these findings and most were very happy with their current home:

> *"I've no plans to move. If I won the lottery I would want to buy this house. I'm very settled here."*
> (Lone parent, south-west)

This respondent went on to say,

> *"I love my house, because I've been in it since it was new, it really feels like my house not the housing association's."*

The commitment to their home was demonstrated by the fact that many had undertaken a considerable amount of work on their homes, not just in terms of decoration or repairs, but also major improvements such as adding new conservatories.

One issue for organisations has been the unpopularity of sheltered housing with one-bedroom in rural areas. A couple of older respondents felt that a spare bedroom was a very positive feature of their bungalow, providing flexibility and enabling their families to visit. In contrast, two respondents mentioned the number of bedrooms in relation to the size of their families as a potential difficulty. These respondents were living in two-bedroom accommodation, and had two young children of different gender. As the children grew up, they would eventually need to move. However, there were only two, three-bedroom properties in the scheme where they were living. Therefore, unless they were very fortunate, they would have to move away. This highlights the potential to offer greater flexibility for households by allowing them to under-occupy larger properties (although this can lead to complications where properties are classed as overlarge for Housing Benefit purposes, and can lead to higher rents for households).

However, whilst most residents were very satisfied with their homes, a small number were critical of the design of the streets outside their home. In particular, criticisms about the use of open grassed areas in front of their houses, or parking areas were common among this group. These residents felt that the design contributed to a lack of privacy and control and could lead to neighbour disputes:

> *"…it's like you're living in a goldfish bowl, and maybe that's added to my feelings of being very vulnerable."*
> (Couple with dependent children, south-east)

> *"What I don't think is very good is this open plan business…it's not so bad now, it's calmed down. Funny enough, when that fence went up – my husband loved nature, you know, being a farmer, he sort of didn't like to be shut in – and he said, 'Do you have to put that fence up', and the foreman, who my husband was very friendly with, said 'You'll be very pleased. You'll thank me one day that that's going up'. And anyhow, three weeks afterwards [husband] said to John, 'Thank goodness you put that fence up. We wouldn't have had any privacy at all'. And, it's not so bad now. It's still bad, but not so bad."*
> (Single older person, south-east)

A small number of residents commented on problems relating to children and teenagers congregating outside their homes. In two instances, residents ruefully noted that the area outside their home was a meeting place not only for teenagers from the village, but also for teenagers who travelled in from surrounding villages to visit their friends:

> *"…in the summer I have all sorts of problems with children hanging around. I think it was a mistake…to make this an open plan area…My mother keeps saying to me 'put nets at your windows'…This is the children coming up to the window and calling their friends. That's how they get covered with finger marks, yeah, Oh, drives me mad. They lean against that wall, that fence, and they jeer across the road at me."*
> (Lone parent, south-east)

As noted earlier, one feature of new schemes is that they can allow some families to group together. However, a couple of respondents stated that they did not think that this was necessarily a positive thing. They suggested that a scheme dominated by one family could exacerbate conflict with other neighbours. In a couple of instances, residents commented on a dispute between themselves and one other neighbour, which escalated very quickly to a dispute between themselves and most of the other neighbours:

"...if you've got a quarrel with one of them, you've got a quarrel with all of them."
(Couple with dependent children, south-east)

A respondent in another scheme echoed this observation where most of the other residents were related to each other:

"...you fall out with one and no-one else speaks to you."
(Couple, south-west)

❏ Home for life or a stepping stone?

Respondents often prefaced their views about home ownership with a statement about having to win the Lottery to have a chance of being able to buy a home, so, as suggested by the longitudinal data, income is an important determinant in moving to owner occupation. Older respondents often felt that they did not want to buy a home at their stage in life, a finding backed by the quantitative analysis above. Either they did not want the burden of a mortgage, or felt that they would not be eligible anyway. Some who had been owner occupiers in the past had been put off this form of tenure because of a bad experience, such as by losing the home when their business failed, or as the consequence of a relationship breakdown. For those who had turned their back on home ownership, or for those who did not have this option, security of tenure was very important:

"...we don't have very many options open. We can, we can go back into private rented accommodation if we want. We could possibly..well we could. We could get something better, but we would have to pay the money and we wouldn't have the security. I think, people, when you're talking about social housing, people think it's mainly young people, it's young families, who are looking for accommodation, but it isn't these days, is it? You've got it right across the board. And I think this is it, I don't think we can afford to do anything else but, you know, stay."
(Couple, south-east)

"...It's a matter of security...the thing we're most concerned with, because we don't have anywhere else to go. And sometimes I think there's an attitude that people in rental housing are only going to be there for six months and then they're going to move on so you don't have to worry about...they'll go on and buy...and we'd like to, but it looks like we're not going to be able to...so...there are still people who need long-term low-cost rental housing. And I think sometimes that's been forgotten."
(Couple, Yorkshire)

Younger respondents had more mixed views. Housing association accommodation was viewed much more as a stepping stone whilst they saved up to try and buy somewhere, either in the village or nearby, again a finding backed by the quantitative analysis. However, whilst some felt certain about wanting to buy a house in the future, others were more circumspect about being able to buy in practice:

> "…it's a dream we all have."
> (Lone parent, Yorkshire)

In contrast, a number of other younger respondents felt that their current home provided a longer-term solution as it enabled them to live in a specific village, often near family and friends. Many of these households with children felt that they would stay where they were, certainly while their children were still at school.

Opportunities for home ownership did vary between the study areas. In the south-east case study, the options open to respondents were severely limited, reflecting a pressured housing market. Indeed, the housing market was so pressured that the policy response in market towns exhibited similar features to rural settlements with regard to the use of strict local connection clauses to ensure housing for households on low-incomes within the town. Respondents in the south-west case study stated that their housing options were affected by the market for holiday and second homes in villages, a view supported by the classification of housing markets in Chapter 2. In contrast, owner occupation was viewed as a more realistic proposition in the case study areas in the north and midlands. However, these options were not necessarily available for households in the village where they lived, but in towns nearby, or in nearby rural areas where there was a lower demand for property.

❑ Moving from social housing to private ownership

One of the major influences on the social rented sector over the past fifteen years has been the introduction of the Right to Buy policy. This is the scheme that allows secure tenants of local authorities and non-charitable housing trusts to buy the house they rent, at a discount of between 32 per cent and 60 per cent for houses and 44 per cent and 70 per cent for flats. Tenants must have rented from their landlord, or another landlord like them, for at least 2 years to qualify for Right to Buy and the property must be their only or main home. There are exceptions to the Right to Buy, such as restrictions on buying sheltered housing or temporary housing. In rural areas its effect has been varied. The housing market classification described in Chapter 2, distinguishes class 1 areas which retained a relatively high level of social housing over the decade 1981-91, from class 2 areas which, starting from a high base of social housing, had lost a substantial proportion by 1991. This section examines longitudinal data (LS) to see how RTB varies according to the characteristics of the occupier and the kind of rural housing market they live in. This is supplemented by the interview data on the views of people living in the social rented sector regarding buying their own home.

The longitudinal datasets give only an indirect view of the characteristics of RTB house purchasers, and in practice RTB cases can be approximated by identifying individuals who had moved from being a social housing tenant to an owner occupier, but had stayed within the same ward. The analysis takes as the 'population at risk' everyone who in the start year was aged 16-74, and was a social housing tenant. It identifies the type of area in which each person lived at the start of the period, along with various other characteristics which may be associated (positively or negatively) with a 'possible RTB' outcome at the end of the period.

Among the LS sample, Table 4 shows a slight, but statistically significant, gender difference, with men more likely to be 'possible RTB' cases. There was also a greater likelihood of RTB among those whose occupation status in 1981 was (semi-)professional or managerial (termed 'higher status' here) as against those with 'lower status' jobs. There was a relationship with the age of the tenants, with people who were already pensioners in 1981, only a third as likely as the young group to be 'possible RTB' cases, those who reached pensionable age during the 1980s around half as likely as those aged 16-24, and with the main family-building group a little more likely than the older group.

Table 4 also shows that people who in 1981 were living in a family (for example a couple with children) or were part of a childless couple were also around twice as likely to be 'possible RTB' than were people living in the parental home, or as a concealed household, or in some other less clear-cut household type. By contrast, those who in 1981 were living alone were noticeably less likely to be 'possible RTB' as the other types of household. The likelihood of lone parent becoming 'possible RTB' was not significantly different from that of the reference group.

Table 4: Characteristics associated with 'possible RTB' among non-migrating adults

	LS (1981 - 1991)	BHPS (1991 - 1998)
At the start of the period: aged 16-74 and a social housing tenant		
reference group characteristic		
urban		
rural class 1	1.13	1.06
rural class 2	1.11	6.66 **
rural class 3	1.21	11.47 **
rural class 4	1.48 **	1.23
rural class 5	1.30 **	2.36 **
rural class 6	1.14	0.01
female		
male	1.14 *	1.03
age 16 - 24		
age 25 - 54	0.60 **	1.00
age 55 - pensionable age	0.49 **	0.23 **
pensionable age - 74	0.34 **	0.17 **
concealed households, living with parents etc.		
single person household	0.65 **	0.24 **
couple without children	1.50 **	3.20 **
lone parent	1.26	0.95
couple with children	2.07 **	0.17 **
occupation of 'lower status'		
occupation of 'higher status'	1.57 **	0.30 **
occupation not known	0.51 **	0.77

Notes:

The values quoted are *odds ratios* (viz: the probability of people with this characteristic experiencing the outcome of interest, over the period covered by that dataset, divided by the equivalent probability of the relevant reference group having that outcome; thus a value of 1.50 for males would indicates that, other things being equal, men are half as likely again to experience that outcome as are women because, of course, females are the relevant reference group here).

** = value significant at the 0.01 level   * = value significant at the 0.05 level

In terms of the rural area classes, Table 4 shows that people living in *any* rural area were more likely to be 'possible RTB' than were equivalent people in urban areas. The differences between the rural area classes' odds ratios are not huge. In particular, there is no strong difference between people in class 1 (continued high social housing) and those in class 2 (declining social housing) where RTB had the most marked impact overall. This somewhat unexpected result suggests that the class 2 areas may include a higher proportion of those groups (such as families and older people) who are most likely to take up RTB wherever they live. So, it follows that it was the nature of the people living locally – the population composition – rather than the characteristics of the place itself which mainly determined local levels of RTB in the 1980s.

Table 4 also presents the results from the equivalent analysis of the BHPS data from the 1990s. In general, rather more caution needs to be exercised in the interpretation of results from the BHPS, due, in particular, to its smaller sample size and greater levels of sample attrition (see Appendix 5). Comparing the BHPS-based analysis of 'possible RTB' with the results from the LS shows a reversal of the finding that being a couple with children, and of having a 'higher status' occupation is related to higher levels of RTB. However, caution may be needed in interpreting results based heavily on the BHPS dataset, especially where – as here – the analysis deals with only a small sub-set (in this case, people who were social housing tenants at the start of the period).

❑ Contact with the RSL and participation

In the main, respondents had a very positive view of housing associations as landlords, in particular how repairs were carried out. Occasionally, respondents were frustrated by the poor quality of work undertaken by builders, requiring repeated repairs and maintenance to the property. In this respect, three respondents felt that they could make a useful contribution to their association in terms of feedback about the relationship between contractors and the association.

Respondents were generally satisfied with the level of contact they had with their landlord. Often they were on first name terms with their managers and liked the personal relationship that they had developed over time. In some instances residents received visits from staff. These residents felt that visits were helpful and contributed to building up a relationship with the association. However, a couple of other residents felt that there was a fine line to be drawn, and that associations should respect their privacy. These respondents liked the fact that the association did not visit unless specifically asked, because they felt that their sense of home would be compromised by repeated visits from the landlord. One respondent reflected on the approach of her own housing association:

"I've got away from that landlord side of it. And it's like you want to settle down and have your own place. If you keep on getting someone knocking at the door, it's like, it takes away that feeling of it's yours. You feel like you're renting again. Whereas they're very good. They give you…you've got space, which is very good…But it's just right, 'cos if, you know, if you've got a problem, they're there at the end of the phone."
(Couple with dependent children, south-east)

In the minority of cases where respondents were less satisfied about repairs, this seemed to be a symptom of poor communication with their landlord. Some respondents noted that the distance between themselves and the association offices precluded personal visits and many were happy to have contact over the phone. Nevertheless, it was felt important that associations handled this form of communication effectively:

"…we'd get through to the receptionist at first, and then you get through to customer service, you know it's all very efficient and modern and 'Oh we'll note it. We'll note it down. We'll get somebody out'. And the worst thing was that when you called again, they denied they ever had the call."
(Couple, Yorkshire)

The DETR (1999) have highlighted a number of difficulties around resident involvement in rural areas. In particular, they note that larger distances, smaller number of properties, and tenant's identification with their own community rather than with their landlord, are barriers to participation.

Respondents had very mixed views about the level of involvement they would prefer. Some respondents felt that they would be interested in having a greater say about the housing association accommodation in their own village:

"We need a voice. Every place, every person needs a voice. It's the only way you're ever going to get anything done."
(Couple with dependent child, east midlands)

A number of associations already had resident forums. However, respondents tended to be unsure about being personally involved in this way because of the distance they would have to travel to attend meetings. Further, representatives often covered a broad geographical area and some respondents felt that they could only really make meaningful comments about their own village. There was little they could contribute for residents living in other villages.

Two respondents stated that they had tried to establish residents' associations within their village, but had met with indifference from the other residents. Reflecting on the potential for a residents' association, a couple of respondents also commented on existing tensions between individuals:

> "…if this development was community minded, then they could be telling the housing association stuff. The trouble is here, there's been…there was a bit of bother, down the end of the road. A family has just moved out. They fell out with everybody."
> (Lone parent, south-east)

> "We eventually got a committee together and I became Chairperson, but then it all fell through…because we were living in each other's pockets at the same time. Because we all had to…I mean you…if someone was a bit awkward about having the grass seeded or whatever, you knew your neighbour and you then had to try and take on a diplomatic role of trying to sort it out without sticking your nose in their affairs…To actually say to them you're not pulling your weight when you've got to hang your washing out with them in the morning, and you know, chat about children and school. It's very hard, and a lot of people got upset by the fact that we were doing all this and they were thinking that the people in [RSL] were just sat on their bums and basically, 'oh this estate is just running itself'. And it wasn't as though we had…you know, they're getting paid and we're sat here running backwards and forwards so…And it caused a lot of fall-outs. It did. There was a lot of fall-outs on this estate."
> (South-west)

A number of respondents noted that there were other means of representation open to them if they felt they needed it. One respondent had recently been in touch with their local councillor to take up an issue with the association over repairs. Others stated that the parish council could be very supportive and help them to represent their views with associations. However, one respondent raised concerns about the extent to which some parish councils represented particular groups within communities.

The issue of tenant participation was also felt by some officers to be a problem. Many RSLs felt there was pressure for tenant participation and were sceptical about its relevance to rural areas. In the south-west, the effects of a failed attempt to set up a tenant management co-op several years ago were still being felt by tenants living on a small cul-de-sac. The housing officer for the patch stressed that although the housing association had learned a lot from the experience they would be very cautious before embarking on similar activity again. Alternatively some argued the need to build much more extensive sets of relations in local communities beyond the tenant base to achieve effective local management.

> *"It's the ongoing management which is really important – often dealing with other individuals and agencies beyond our tenants and this is also what costs – the hidden add-ons."*
> (RSL, east midlands)

CHAPTER 4

LIVING IN A RURAL AREA

Housing is only one of the issues that characterise rural life. Transport, employment and access to services are also often highlighted as problems for rural dwellers, as is the way in which these factors intertwine so that none can be isolated as the one problem that needs to be addressed. This is the case with housing in rural areas, the demand for which and the provision of which are influenced by a series of other issues. This chapter uses both the quantitative analysis of national data from Census and longitudinal studies, and the interview material from the five case study areas, to look at how these elements combine in terms of social housing.

❑ Commuting patterns

Limited rural employment opportunities are often influenced by the need for affordable social housing, as will be seen below. One question which arises from the link between housing and employment is the extent to which a lengthy journey to work has become an inevitable feature of rural labour markets.

Table 5 examines variations in commuting patterns between the rural housing market types. The one marked contrast between the rural area classes is an expected one, in that the 'commuter villages' of class 3 and class 4 have a strong linkage to large neighbouring cities, in marked contrast to the more remote class 5 and class 6 areas. Class 1 has high continued levels of social housing – including some former mining villages – which are most commonly associated with problems of access to employment (Cartmel and Furlong, 2000). Table 5 suggests that the lost local jobs in these areas have not led to high levels of long-distance commuting, probably due to the people affected either remaining unemployed or moving away to find work.

Table 5: Where rural area residents worked (1991)

Workers living in:	percent who work in:		
	a rural area	smaller urban area	large urban area
Class 1	56	20	24
Class 2	56	19	25
Class 3	43	19	38
Class 4	42	15	42
Class 5	63	20	17
Class 6	61	20	19
All rural areas	**50**	**19**	**30**

Table 6: Dependence on urban area jobs, by occupation group (1991)

Workers living in:	percent who work in an urban area:			
	professionals and managers	other white collar	manufacturing workers	other (including agricultural)
Class 1	51	47	40	29
Class 2	54	48	35	21
Class 3	65	60	43	29
Class 4	65	61	49	28
Class 5	44	42	29	16
Class 6	46	45	32	15
All rural areas	**51**	**54**	**48**	**34**

Commuting patterns vary substantially between different groups of workers, so it is important to assess how far the availability of jobs in urban areas is restricted to those groups whose pay levels are likely to be high enough to make longer-distance commuting a practical option. Table 6 addresses this question by calculating – for each rural area class – the proportion of four broad groups of workers employed in urban rather than rural areas. All the occupation groups show the same restricted level of commuting to urban areas from the remoter class 5 and class 6 areas. As for class 1 areas, less well-paid workers are rather more dependent on jobs in rural areas than are their class 2 counterparts, (where levels of social housing have declined). It may be that at least part of the employment difficulties in class 1 areas is due to the decline in local rural job opportunities (for example, coal mining) on which they were dependent.

In practice, an area's labour market prospects reflect conditions in the area itself as well as those in areas near enough to be accessible for commuters. A GIS-based 'surfacing' analysis has been used here to compare areas in terms of the overall level of job opportunities in and around any ward. Table 7 reveals the result that residents of class 3 areas (close to urban centres) have a level of job access that is half of the average for all England's urban areas, including areas as rich in job opportunities as central London. The result here for class 1 areas shows them to be around the average value for England's rural areas overall, but of course the data here cannot show a decline over time in local job opportunities.

Table 7: Access to job opportunities (percent of England average)

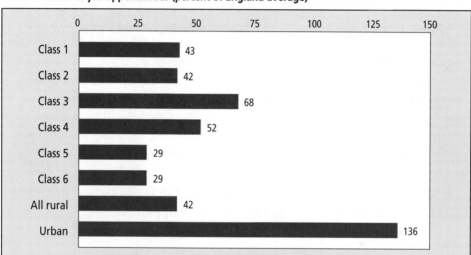

Table 8: Change in access to job opportunities 1981-1991 (percent of England average)

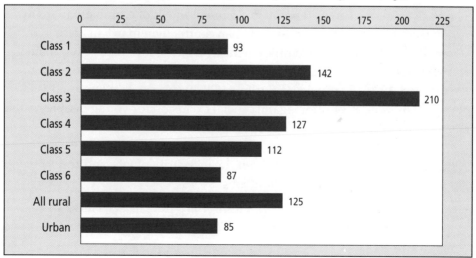

The same job access analysis has been applied to 1981 as well as to 1991 data on job opportunities, to highlight those areas around which job losses have outweighed any local job growth (Coombes and Raybould, 2000). Table 8 shows the results of this analysis of change in levels of local job opportunities from 1981 to 1991 with, once again, the value for each type of area standardised against the national average value. The principal result is in accordance with the findings of Illouz-Winicki and Paillard (1998) from many western countries: rural areas have seen stronger job growth than have towns and cities. At the same time, there is clear evidence that class 1 areas have suffered declining levels of local job opportunities, but a surprising finding is that class 6 areas (low levels of social housing, high numbers of retirees, low constraint on new build) experienced a still higher rate of job loss. A key reason will be that the overall growth in local job opportunities for rural areas largely reflects employment 'suburbanisation' out from towns and cities. Table 8 shows that whilst urban areas have fared worst in maintaining their employment levels, there is particularly high growth nearby for the class 4 and, most especially, class 3 'commuter village' areas. The other interesting feature of Table 8 is that class 2 areas have performed very well, despite not being particularly well located to benefit from suburbanisation. It is not clear why these areas' distinctiveness – identified here purely in terms of housing characteristics, and in particular a high level of RTB in the 1980s – should be associated with strong growth in the level of job opportunities.

❑ Jobs and housing: the experience of occupiers

The analysis above shows that unemployment is less of a problem in many rural areas, especially those near an urban centre, than in urban areas themselves. However, rural employment tends to be low-paid (Chapman *et al*, 1998) and insecure, seasonal and part-time in nature (Joseph Rowntree Foundation, 1999). Cartmel and Furlong, (2000) suggest that low-paid employment is no protection against social exclusion for young people, in the face of housing shortages and transport problems.

A number of respondents talked about the insecurity of jobs and the likelihood of having to find different jobs:

> *"...how many all year round jobs can there be in a place that is, I don't know... it's supported by the holiday industry, so it can't have all year round jobs."*
> (South-west)

Another respondent stated that the level of insecurity in the job market encouraged him to rent rather than buy a home:

> *"I couldn't afford a mortgage. It would scare me to death. If I lose my job tomorrow, I've got a certain amount of back up that my rent will be paid. I won't get kicked out. That's my safety net. This to me is safety."*
> (Couple with dependent child, south-east)

A feature of respondents' comments was the separation of the location of housing from employment. A couple of respondents had moved to a village where they worked, but had subsequently lost their jobs and found alternative work elsewhere. Most were pragmatic about the need to commute, either to find work or to maintain their current jobs, and this pragmatism perhaps reflected the type of work available. Most stated that ownership of a car was often essential to fit together housing with employment and access to services and facilities.

Owning, or having access to, a car was crucial for the respondents and influenced the extent to which they felt settled, whether they had local ties to the area or not. Very few of the respondents did not have cars. Of those who did not, one respondent felt that the bus service was adequate for her needs. Others were far less settled, and felt isolated and wanted to move:

> *"…it's just me personally would like to get out of the village, you know, because, I feel I'm not in a position to buy a car, you know, at the moment. And I just feel very isolated, you know. And that in itself can be a bad thing come winter-time or for anybody really. You know, you become a bit brain dead don't you. You do though don't you? You feel isolated. You want to go out, but you can't go out 'cos there's nowhere to go apart from a pub and a club. You don't want to take your daughter to things like that, you need things around you that's going to stimulate you both. And there ain't that here."*
> (Lone parent, east midlands)

Another issue facing couples was that often one partner required the car, meaning that the other had to rely on public transport. Some respondents noted that this could cause problems for whoever did not have access to a car. In one instance, moving to a village with poor public transport had resulted in one partner of a couple giving up his job because he was unable to commute, and since then had been unable to find work nearby.

Migration to and from rural England

Table 9: Net migration rate 1990-1 (percent)

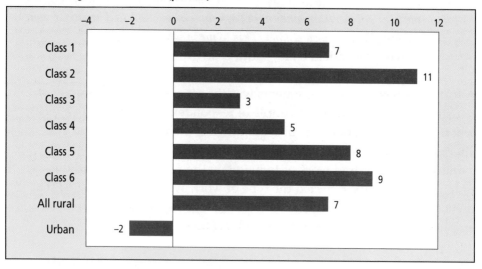

Growth or decline in local job opportunities may not have a direct impact on local unemployment levels: there are a number of other factors which influence this, in particular the net migration to or from the area by people seeking work. Table 9 presents a net migration analysis showing how many more in-migrants there were to each housing market class than were out-migrants from it, as a percentage of the out-migration flow. Thus the value of -2 for urban areas means there were only 98 in-migrants for every 100 out-migrants in 1990-1 (with migrants within and between urban areas not figuring in this calculation). The job growth of class 2 areas – shown in Table 8 – can be seen in Table 9 to have been associated with a strong net in-migration flow. Unfortunately only one year's migration data is available, so it is impossible to explore whether the in-migration was a response to job growth in these areas or whether it had been underway for some time and had itself fuelled the growth of economic activity.

It is worth noting here that some of the migration patterns of 1990-1 are known to be unlike most of the 1980s or 1990s with respect to north-south flows. The house price slump at the end of the 1980s produced a temporary reversal of the long-standing net flow from the north to south and this can be seen clearly in Table 9's otherwise surprising higher net in-flows to class 4 and class 6 – which are very largely in the north – than to class 3 and class 5 which are mainly in the south. This is also part of the explanation for the surprisingly strong net in-migration to class 1 areas, because there will have been some suppression of the long-standing flow of out-migration from these economically disadvantaged areas towards the south. The level of in-migration to such areas is not so readily explained, and other evidence is needed to help explain this pattern.

Table 10 may provide a contribution to this explanation, because it explores the 1990-1 migration data to identify where the in-migrants had come from. Although the differences between area types are modest – apart from the expected strong in-flows from large urban areas to 'commuter villages' in class 3 and class 4 – one finding is that migration to class 1 areas tends to be from other rural areas. This pattern is consistent with the possibility that the greater housing availability, including social housing, in class 1 areas attracts in-movers from other rural areas within the same locality which have more constrained housing markets.

Table 10: Where migrants to rural areas came from (1990-91)

	percent who came from:		
Migrants to:	**a rural area**	**smaller urban area**	**large urban area**
Class 1	61	16	21
Class 2	56	18	24
Class 3	44	20	34
Class 4	48	15	33
Class 5	56	19	23
Class 6	58	17	23
All rural areas	**53**	**18**	**27**

Table 11 shows that the pattern of out-flows from rural areas is remarkably similar to that of in-flows in terms of the relative strengths of linkages with urban as against rural areas. As a result, the best portrayal of this pattern is of a variation in the intensity of migration exchanges between types of areas, because the net flow is always a low proportion of the overall flows involved. These analyses were repeated for separate age groups and show a very great stability across all groups in these patterns of migration exchange. Even the young adult group, who are most likely to migrate to rather than from urban areas, differ only by a couple of percentage points from the broad pattern of values which Tables 9 and 10 present.

Table 11: Where migrants from rural areas went to live (1990-1)

Migrants from:	percent who went to live in:		
	a rural area	smaller urban area	large urban area
Class 1	63	17	18
Class 2	61	19	19
Class 3	48	22	27
Class 4	52	17	29
Class 5	60	20	17
Class 6	62	18	17
All rural areas	57	19	21

❑ Mixed communities: occupiers' views on their place in the village

The analysis above shows that there is significant movement in and out of rural communities, and that a high level of social housing may contribute to people from other rural areas moving into a new village, as well as the familiar pattern of urban and suburban dwellers moving to rural areas within commuting distance of towns. This migration can present problems for rural settlements with existing residents having to adjust to relatively high numbers of new residents moving in. This can be compounded if the incomers are moving into social housing, as discussed in relation to the issues of residualisation and low demand in Chapter 1.

People living in social housing in rural areas had a range of views about the extent of integration and participation with the broader community. Respondents who had lived in a particular settlement for a number of years tended to feel that the sense of community had altered for the worse over time. Respondents commented on turnover of population, with new people moving into villages, and young people tending to move away. One respondent felt that opportunities for people to get to know each other within the village had diminished as facilities where people met each other such as shops and pubs had closed down. Sometimes respondents noted the exclusive nature of the community they lived in,

> "...it was like a dream come true, really...to get something like this, I mean in this village. I mean it's a very expensive village. A lot of people, commuters and that live here, and the prices...I would never be able to afford a house in this

village, you know, unless I became mega rich. And I'm quite proud to be here, apart from my neighbours…I feel quite honoured to be here."
(Couple with dependent children, south-east)

Respondents generally seemed less concerned about fitting into the village as a whole and instead placed greater emphasis on their own family or network of friends, or upon their own household:

"I'm not into all that community crap."
(Couple with dependent children, Yorkshire)

In reflecting on their circumstances and the potential for feeling isolated, such respondents stressed that their home was the focus of their lives, rather than the settlement in which they lived, so that even if they did not know many people, it did not matter to them. On the other hand, a resident who had moved from the midlands to the south-west reflected the diversity of views on this subject:

"…there is a lot of community spirit. I've been adopted as one of the locals."
(Lone parent, south-west)

A number of respondents spoke about how the association development fitted in with the broader village. Generally the respondents who were living in the village at the time the development was being built noted that there tended to be a broad concern over who was going to be housed in housing association schemes in villages. One respondent commented on local press reports that the new housing estate where she lived would result in problem families being imported into the village by the housing association,

"…they were worried that it was going to be a noisy, child-ridden community, which it isn't."
(Couple with dependent children, south-west)

❏ Overall well-being

Living in a rural area is generally thought to offer a better quality of life and even better health than for urban dwellers. People living in rural areas often report that these factors outweigh the disadvantages of living in the countryside. This perception can be examined by an analysis of the longitudinal data (see Appendix 5).

The BHPS (for the 1990s only) gives information on whether people are "living comfortably" or at least "doing alright" in terms of their economic well-being in general. This shows that people in social rented housing are less than a third as likely as owner occupiers to answer positively to this question (there was a similar but less extreme contrast with the 'higher'/'lower' status distinction) and this applies to rural areas as much as urban ones. There is no significant difference between non-migrants and migrants, despite the evidence discussed above that the migrant group tends to be more affluent. There is no consistent urban-rural contrast in the results, and the difference between the classes of rural areas is not great.

People's self-declared health state may as much reflect feelings about their well-being in general as well as about their health more specifically. The BHPS provides data on whether people felt their health to be 'average' (or better) than that of most people their age. Table 12 (left-hand side) shows that people didn't fully 'standardise' for their age when answering, because fewer older people felt their health to be no worse than was to be expected at their age. The other differentials in Table 12 do tend to reflect genuine health differentials: a much higher likelihood of better health among those in 'higher status' occupations; worse health of those in social housing (perhaps mainly due to social housing including more poor people); and living in a couple proving to be conducive to good health.

However, while clearly housing tenure and socio-economic status are important regardless of location, it is worth noting the geographical effects on health and well-being. Migrating from rural to urban areas has a clear negative association, whilst moving in the other direction is notably beneficial (moving within either urban or rural areas has no significant effect, compared to not moving at all). Most remarkably, all the rural area classes are significantly 'more healthy' than urban areas, with the exception of class 1, where the chances of feeling healthy are significantly lower, perhaps associated with the relatively high unemployment found in these areas.

Table 12 (right-hand side) also shows the characteristics of those content with the neighbourhood in which they live. There is a strong contrast between the dissatisfaction of rural migrants to urban areas and the contentment of urban migrants to rural areas. Neighbourhood satisfaction seems to peak before retirement, having dipped when people were at child-rearing age. The very strong dissatisfaction of lone parents may, of course, reflect a deeper feeling of discontent, but they could also be expressing unease about how some

Table 12: Characteristics associated with other aspects of well-being

	BHPS (1991 - 1998)	
At the start of the period:	Feeling healthy	Liking neighbourhood
reference group characteristic		
urban		
rural class 1	0.58**	1.69**
rural class 2	1.21**	0.92
rural class 3	1.64**	1.81**
rural class 4	1.62**	2.95**
rural class 5	1.33**	1.94**
rural class 6	1.21**	1.29*
age 16-24		
age 25 - 54	0.71**	0.81**
age 55 - pensionable age	0.70**	1.45**
pensionable age - 74	0.48**	1.18
female		
male	0.91**	0.97
concealed households, living with parents etc.		
single person household	1.30**	1.36**
couple without children	1.35**	0.87*
lone parent	1.12	0.34**
couple with children	1.32**	0.94
owner occupied household		
social rented	0.65**	0.69**
other	1.01	0.86*
occupation of 'lower status'		
occupation of 'higher status'	1.48**	1.30**
occupation not known	0.73**	0.82**
non-migrants		
rural → rural migrants	1.03	1.54**
rural → urban migrants	0.83**	0.67**
urban → rural migrants	1.26**	1.77**
urban → urban migrants	1.11	1.03
** = value significant at the 0.01 level	* = value significant at the 0.05 level	

neighbours react to them. With the exception of residents of class 2 areas, where levels of social housing have dropped over the 90s, people in rural areas are more likely to be happy with their neighbourhoods than are urban residents, echoing the findings of Burrows and Rhodes (1998). The variation between the rural area classes is not easy to explain, but it is striking that residents of class 1 – despite their various problems which have been described here – register a level of satisfaction with where they live which is close to the average for England's rural areas.

To summarise, the study has found that rural areas are less affected by unemployment than urban areas, but that is largely due to relatively well-paid workers commuting out of the area to nearby urban centres. People without a car in a village can often be unable to work at all, or feel trapped in their surroundings. Migration into rural areas is strongest in areas close to urban settlements, as would be expected and one interesting finding is that migration from other rural areas is strong where there is good availability of social housing, suggesting this may be an attraction to rural dwellers with poorer housing provision in their area. New social housing and the arrival of new residents was not generally welcomed by existing residents, who tended to be apprehensive about the impact of the development. New residents without family ties in the area did not feel it important to be part of the community, but put greatest emphasis on their family as the social unit.

Having said that, the satisfaction of people living in rural areas is high, even in areas of high unemployment and the effect of moving from an urban to a rural area is a positive one.

CHAPTER 5

PROVIDING RURAL HOUSING

This section of the report highlights key issues surrounding the delivery and management of rural social housing schemes. It summarises the main themes emerging from organisational interviews conducted across the five case study areas. Interestingly, most RSLs included in the study had recently undergone or were in the process of internal review, often exploring the overall direction and priorities of the organisation. These reviews can be seen as linked concerns about the local delivery and management of rural schemes with broader questions regarding the future role and purpose of social housing.

❑ Delivering rural social housing

Though nationally there is generally thought to be an undersupply of rural social housing, the case studies have been selected on the basis of contrasting housing market situations so there should be differences between them in the nature and level of demand for social housing. There is also evidence from within individual case study areas of contrasting patterns of demand emerging due to the highly localised nature of housing markets. There is often a perception of a growing polarisation between areas of very acute demand and other areas where demand is falling away.

Such differences reflect the varied role that rural social housing plays both within and between different areas. In some areas demand had fallen off so that the rural social housing stock was being used to house almost exclusively the unemployed, leading one officer in the north-west to comment:

> "...people in employment do not rent social housing."

But this contrasted with other areas and schemes where the majority of tenants were in employment such as in the south-east. However, even within the south-east, where there was a particularly high level of employed tenants, significant variations between the individual schemes were noted.

Unsurprisingly, localised polarisation of the housing market is compounded further in national parks or Areas of Outstanding Natural Beauty (AONB). In the example of the north-west case study – part of which falls within national park boundaries – some villages are experiencing steady increases in house prices while demand for property in nearby villages falls away; such that the local housing strategy refers to this polarisation as the 'two faces of the borough'.

At the regional scale, one RSL in Yorkshire was keen that low demand in some of the conurbations should not obscure the acute shortages in some rural locations. Such varied contexts raise difficult issues for housing strategy and expose the difficulties of attempting to construct regional or even local authority-wide, strategic agendas. Whilst organisations were acutely sensitive to these differences in the character of the local housing markets, there was a general sense that their ability to respond strategically to this situation was limited by the grant allocation systems. For a number of RSLs, the central issue in the provision of affordable social housing was the lack of geographical sensitivity in the grant system and in the Total Cost Indicators (TCI)[1] to provide affordable social housing in areas of unmet demand. It was perceived that these problems were compounded in national park areas where lobbying continues for higher grant rates.

❑ Rural housing shortage and dislocation

There was evidence of a rural housing shortage and that those not in waged employment, or on low or middle incomes, are being dislocated from their local communities through prohibitive house prices and a lack of affordable social housing opportunities.

In the east midlands case study area the perceived situation is of serious under-provision of social housing and, given development pressures, few

---

1   The Total Cost Indicator (TCI) is the fixed percentage grant rates and guideline capital costs set by the Housing Corporation, which vary according to type of project and region.

opportunities to redress the balance. Within some particularly 'desirable' locations in the south-east case study area there was evidence that ex-council housing sold under RTB is supplying the second homes market. This loss of social housing has not just been confined to RTB on local authority stock but also includes, in some areas, a significant loss of older housing association stock built 30-40 years ago. In parts of the north-west and south-west case studies, holiday lets formed a substantial proportion of the rural housing stock and one interviewee referred to there being a global market for homes in the area.

In areas of high demand and high property prices, such as the class 3 and 5 areas, social housing forms an important route into housing and may be the only affordable option for those on low and modest incomes leading to long tenancies and low turnover of properties. In the south-west, one RSL argued that the security and quality of their accommodation meant that:

> "...people don't tend to move out of social housing – we just don't get the turnover. When people do move it is generally for other reasons such as employment or family."

❏ Young people and rural social housing

An issue at the heart of concern over rural housing availability is the movement of young people out of rural areas because of difficulty in finding accommodation when they want to leave the parental home. There is a view that providing more social housing in villages would allow more young people to make this transition from their parental home without moving away to towns or cities.

Analysis of the quantitative data (Table 13) does confirm that a higher proportion of urban areas' population is in their 20s, and it is also the case that through the 1980s all types of rural area saw a net decline in the proportion of their residents who were in their 20s, at a time when this age group was growing, possibly reflecting rural young people moving to urban areas (whether or not this was primarily for housing reasons). In 1981, the rural areas with most social housing – class 1 and class 2 – also had a higher proportion of young adults than did other rural areas, but the fastest fall in numbers of young people is also in class 1 areas which should have been able to retain young people if social housing provision were the main factor in their moving away. These areas have experienced a strong decline in

Table 13: Percent of population in 1981 and 1991 aged 20-29

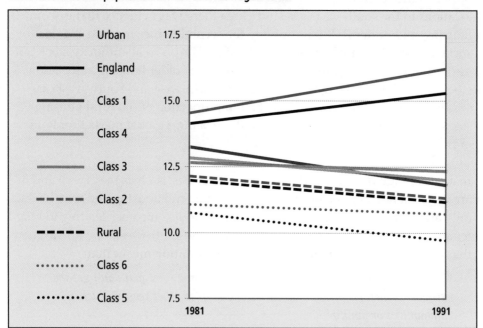

employment opportunities, as discussed in Chapter 4 and this non-housing factor may be the most influential reason for young people to move away. The fact that class 3 areas, where housing markets are under the most pressure, have seen the slowest decline in numbers of young adults also suggests that housing factors are not the over-riding influence on youth migration.

Table 14 contrasts LS data on the experience over 10 years of young people aged 12 to 15 (as at 1981), with BHPS data on transitions over a period of 7 years for 16-24 year olds (as at 1991)[2]. Again, the LS analysis does find that class 1 is the most favourable location for young people to make the transition to a separate household, but the BHPS analysis gives a strongly contrasting result, again suggesting that housing is not the main reason why young people move away from rural areas.

Both datasets also show that young women have a higher probability of setting up their own household than young men, which reflects young women's lower average age on leaving their parental home (DETR, 1999).

---

2   There are technical difficulties which arise when trying to compare results from the BHPS and the LS described in Appendix 4

Table 14: Characteristics associated with household formation by young people

	LS (1981 - 1991)	BHPS (1991 - 1998)
At the start of the period:	# aged 12-15	# aged 16-24
reference group characteristic		
urban		
rural class 1	1.84 **	0.63
rural class 2	1.40	2.01 **
rural class 3	1.20	1.03
rural class 4	1.35	2.56 **
rural class 5	1.17	0.61
rural class 6	1.60 *	1.61
female		
male	0.50 **	0.27 **
owner occupied household		
social rented	1.37 **	0.73
other	0.93	0.77
occupation of 'lower status'		
occupation of 'higher status'	0.58 **	1.25
occupation not known	0.72 *	0.94
non-migrants		
rural → rural migrants	6.30 **	18.61 **
rural → urban migrants	11.14 **	23.45 **
urban → rural migrants	13.64 **	9.42 **
urban → urban migrants	13.85 **	10.03 **

excluding those who become lone parents by the end of the period

** = value significant at the 0.01 level   * = value significant at the 0.05 level

The principal finding in Table 14 – on which the LS and BHPS differ only in emphasis – is that being a migrant is the characteristic most strongly associated with household formation. This result echoes the in-depth study of Rugg and Jones (1999) who found very few rural young people who had succeeded in starting their own household in their home area, which may mean that too strict an interpretation of local connections requirements may be counterproductive if mobility is as important to young people in rural areas as these findings suggest.

This evidence suggests that young peoples' prospects of early household formation do not vary strongly across the country, but the limited differences which have emerged identify the mainly northern classes of rural areas as offering a somewhat better chance of transition from the parental home. However, the key factor that makes this transition more likely is not where young people lived initially, it is being willing and able to move to another rural area.

The degree to which agencies viewed the movement of young people out of rural areas as a problem varied, as did the attitude of individual officers. For some, the enforced move to urban locations by young people was regarded as almost inevitable and, not necessarily, a negative outcome given the potential there for new employment and social opportunities. In contrast, others, including an independent rural housing enabler in the north-west, felt very strongly that housing providers had not even attempted to address the needs of young people in rural areas. One local councillor expressed a similar sentiment:

> "...my ward is a very poor rural village and the biggest problem is for young people. I don't think they are catered for, but it is very difficult."

These comments were reinforced by evidence from an RSL operating in the same area expressing reservations about letting to young single people given past experience:

> "...we struggle to let because we don't necessarily want to let them to young singles who will trash them within six months of it being let – having had experience of that a few times."
> (RSL, north-west)

However, strong views were also expressed about the need to prevent the further exodus of young people, often linked to broader arguments about the need to ensure the survival of rural communities.

❑ Falling demand

The issue of falling demand co-existed with problems of undersupply. In addition to individuals being pushed out of their communities of origin by shortages of social housing, there was also a sense in which whole rural communities were becoming dislocated in parts of the north-west, south-west and Yorkshire case studies. A local authority rural housing enabler in the north-west summed up the scenario of physically isolated communities comprised of vulnerable people with poor access to services:

> *"…we will end up with a small remaining nucleus of people in social housing who are benefit dependent with the most acute needs."*

In the north-west case study, structural unemployment has resulted in some isolated rural stock being difficult to let, hence various means are being used to try to fill the vacant stock including radio advertising. Here the problems of RSLs finding potential tenants has been exacerbated by the Large Scale Voluntary Transfer in the district which for other RSLs has led to a switch from having 100 per cent local authority nominations to none. Despite preparing for this change, officers felt that any vacancies in some villages had become 'a nightmare'. Even so they remained reluctant to house certain groups who were deemed more likely to engage in anti-social behaviour.

Low and falling demand was perceived as a problem in some sites across all the case studies, though in general long tenancies mean this has not as yet translated into high void figures. In the south-east, for example, falling demand for some of the older, poorer quality stock had surprised housing association officers. Thus even in high demand areas, those that are able are exercising preferences which may increase the sense of a hierarchy within the rural social housing sector. Whilst a number of RSLs, for example in the north-west, east midlands and south-east, were investing in refurbishment programmes there was also a fear that such 'rejuvenation' activities might make properties more vulnerable to RTB. In the east midlands, stock rejuvenation was linked by an RSL to the need to re-image the whole social housing sector towards 'community housing'.

A common problem across the case study areas was the difficulty of letting housing designed specifically for elderly people – in particular one-bedroom sheltered accommodation which, one officer claimed,

> *"…we can't get rid of for love or money."*

Hence various schemes are under way to remould this stock, responding to the norms elderly people have about their housing requirements. The general notion of changing norms and offering tenants and potential tenants greater choice seems central to the future of the social housing tenure. However, the idea of re-inventing social housing to fit a more flexible 'community housing' model, complete with increased tenant mobility, is seriously undermined by the limited desirability of much existing stock.

❑ Scheme development and the planning framework

Moving from the identification of need to actual scheme development involves negotiating a number of barriers. For example, in practice new schemes may not be of adequate scale to meet the actual needs present in a village because of concerns about the impact and acceptability of a social housing development, leading one RSL to comment that:

> "...with our most recent scheme we could have filled it three times over...but there are going to be problems if you try to build a large estate in a village. The people we house often have a range of other problems in addition to their housing need and big schemes just create a recipe for disaster."

Another source of tension can be agreeing the exact location of schemes within villages, even where there is local support in principle for the scheme to be developed. One scheme in the south-east had the active support of the parish council until specific sites were proposed by the RSL:

> "...you wouldn't believe the prejudice and bigotry...there has been uproar and the tensions reverberate over a very long period. Wherever a site touches the edge of private housing you can anticipate a big row."

Similar prejudice was also encountered where attempts were made to secure affordable social housing as one element within private sector led developments. As a result, many of the schemes examined in the study were adjacent to pre-existing local authority schemes, often on the edge of the villages. However, one perception shared across the case studies and summed up by an RSL in the south-west was that, 'all the easy schemes have now been done'. This in part may explain why alternative modes of rural social housing provision are becoming of increasing interest. This includes the purchase by RSLs of existing properties, either in good condition (known as Existing Satisfactory Purchase), or requiring some repair short of full rehabilitation (which is termed Purchase and Repair). There was general sense of optimism with regard to this method as a vehicle for meeting rural housing need with one interviewee commenting:

> "...we're almost going out and shopping to order."
> (RSL, Yorkshire)

Whilst generally viewed as a good way of providing rural social housing with the advantages over new developments of shorter delivery times, not altering the fabric of villages and being less susceptible to stigmatisation, there were also some significant difficulties. A serious limitation to the use of purchase in some places was the prohibitive cost of local houses, making it financially unworkable given the Total Cost Indicators. This was particularly the case in the south-east and east midlands cases. However, one local authority was using capital receipts to fund purchases above Purchase and Repair cash limits.

Purchase can also help to fuel local housing markets. One RSL in the south-east expressed concern that their interest in buying was helping to inflate local house prices and was exacerbated by RSLs competing against each other for properties – though in some places partnership working was being used to reduce competition. A related concern was that purchase might limit the housing options for local people and existing RSL tenants looking to move into owner occupancy. One local authority in Yorkshire sought to address these concerns by targeting only properties vacant for over six months. Fears were also expressed over the potentially poorer quality of accommodation delivered through this mechanism.

Purchase of existing stock by RSLs can provoke local opposition. One RSL in the south-east found that a Purchase and Repair project had provoked prejudice amongst neighbouring owner occupiers who,

> "...have a real fear of a tenant living next door."

In Yorkshire one RSL claimed,

> "...adjoining properties can be horrified when they hear that we have bought the property."

However, the cost factor remains perhaps the most significant barrier, even if grant levels were to increase to respond to some regional increases, it may not be possible to keep up quickly enough. Given these problems a local authority in the south-east argued that their rural work in future was likely to centre on making better use of their existing stock.

❑ Scheme financing

The gap between the level of central government subsidy and the costs of delivering rural social housing has grown. Moreover, in rural areas the absence of a large stock built up over time, limits the scope to operate rent pools. The need for private sector borrowing to fund development has also led to a problem regarding Mortgagee in Possession clauses. These give private lenders the option to dispose of properties on the market as a last resort to cover unpaid loans, and can conflict with local connection conditions attached to the occupancy of rural social housing. The recent PPG3 (DETR 2000) re-asserts that Mortgagee in Possession clauses should not be necessary to secure private loans. However, lenders may be resistant to offering loan without Mortgagee in Possession clauses and for that reason they may be favoured by RSLs:

> *"…the Mortgagee in Possession exclusion clause makes it easier to raise private finance and we would rather not go ahead without this – we need it. The new PPG3 has an especially bad impact for small, rural HAs. There is a need for a more pragmatic line – it makes development more expensive – so how will this shortfall be covered?"*
> (RSL, south-west)

Other financial barriers stem from the pursuit of Best Value, which means local authorities are no longer selling their land at low prices and are increasingly looking to obtain market value. Thus one HA officer remarked,

> *"How does this square with whole notion of providing affordable housing?"*

❑ Managing the rural housing stock

A central theme of the research was to ascertain who is being given priority through the allocation system. For many organisations the issue of rural allocations was perceived as being especially sensitive:

> *"We are a specialist organisation supplying rural housing – recognising that to meet needs in the rural context you need a different approach – you have to overcome the NIMBY factor."*
> (RSL, south-west)

The issue of gatekeepers emerged as a difficult, but important, aspect of rural social housing, with parish councils often playing an active role. Re-assurances that 'problem families' will not be 'imported' to live in the schemes are often a key part of this negotiation process. Yet, the imperative for the HA to work to restrictive financial frameworks and meet local authority nomination rights may undermine the degree to which they are able to screen potential tenants. There was concern that the credibility of the

RSL amongst local people rests on the nominations made by the local authority and that maintaining credibility in villages and delivering workable schemes requires a degree of flexibility, or screening, in the allocation process. One RSL manager emphasised the difficult but important task of retaining control and responsibility over allocations decisions:

> "...other organisations sometimes don't help themselves by passing over responsibility for allocations to the district council. If they do this they don't have a chance if decisions are challenged."

Some interviewees felt that operating a waiting list independently of the local authority could facilitate a more sensitive approach to lettings. This was regarded as particularly useful in situations where local authorities appear too rigid in their nominations and present RSLs with a *fait accompli* that may hinder attempts to establish sustainable communities. This can emerge as a tension between RSLs working to a local lettings policy and the local authority working to needs-based criteria.

There were differences in the attitude of RSLs to 'social engineering' in allocations policies. Some RSLs felt that it was very important to try to avoid the moral decision-making about who the 'deserving' are:

> "...from our experience even those branded 'undeserving' will settle in."
> (RSL, south-west)

However, others were more explicitly engaged in social engineering, which they defended on the grounds that RSLs were morally accountable for the effects of their schemes:

> "...we can chat informally with the local authority and say send us someone decent."
> (RSL, south-east)

The latter quote also demonstrates how informal practices may be privileged over formal policy and procedures. Attempts were being made, though, to formalise a 'balanced' approach. In the south-east, one officer remarked that their re-drafted policies would emphasise flexibility and balancing housing needs against local connection. In Yorkshire, one RSL reported that their new lettings policy would allow more sensitivity to local circumstances by bringing together three components: needs, economic connection and social connection. The belief of many interviewees was that processes have become more transparent assisted by clearer communication with the parish council.

"I am quite willing to go along to public meetings and defend our decisions... clarity and openness has paid dividends. It is also important that communities don't feel that schemes have been imposed upon them. We actively involve the parish council without letting them make the decisions...so we might discuss designs and initial lettings. The process of letting them know seems to work very well."
(RSL, south-west)

Some interviewees stressed that the role which social housing plays may change over time. Whilst the initial scheme allocations may perform a particular role at the outset, subsequent re-lets might lead to a different use of the housing. A number of associations stressed a shift in focus away from meeting need towards meeting a broader range of demand as they reposition themselves to play a more active role in 'making communities'. This aligns with emergent agendas about re-shaping the future of the social housing sector away from the 'tenure of last resort'. However, there was a feeling that some local authorities had been slow to grasp this shift in emphasis towards developing a 'community housing' agenda.

❏ Management systems

The overwhelming characteristic of rural schemes was the labour intensive nature of management due to the dispersed stock. This however was counter balanced by the perception that the scale and degree of management problems was generally far less than in urban settings. Overall there were wide variations in the degree and manner of contact with tenants. This varied from organisations that sought regular contact and so were very keen, for example, to maintain door-to-door rent collection or regular monthly visits, and those who waited to hear from the tenants. One housing association reported that some of their rural tenants 'make do' for themselves – often getting repairs done and then sending them the bill. However, in one example from the east midlands, this 'arms length' style of management adopted by the RSL was felt by tenants to be inadequate, in that the RSL had withdrawn from more intensive estate management whilst the tenants reported ongoing problems on the scheme.

Highlighted in the interviews was a sense that specialist rural RSLs have the experience and are much better positioned to manage the rural stock. There was therefore some resistance to the large, general needs associations taking on rural housing work. In the east midlands case study the local authority also identified the separation of development and management functions within the larger RSL as potentially problematic:

> "...the link between the development and management aims are critical; problems occur when the left hand doesn't know what the right hand is doing. There needs to be work on the management before the 11th hour."

One strategy for avoiding potential management problems was the use of exclusion clauses for anti-social behaviour being introduced by some RSLs. In one case this had been induced by the fear that they would expose themselves to problems without it:

> "...we don't want to be the only landlord left who will take people excluded by everybody else."
> (RSL, north-west)

A central management theme to emerge was meeting the range of tenants' support needs in isolated rural communities. In some cases specialist floating support teams had been established to fill the gap between housing providers and social services and closer working relations were developing with social services. However, in one case there were some significant political barriers.

> "...there is a political perception that this is a 'nice' place to be and there can be a pressure to keep problems off the agenda so we don't jeopardise tourism."
> (RSL, south-west)

❑ Housing Plus

Since the launch of the Housing Plus initiative by the Housing Corporation in 1995, there has been growing encouragement to look in more depth at quality of life issues. However, some commentators have highlighted the difficulty of translating Housing Plus concepts to rural areas (Oldfield King, 1997). Evidence from across the case studies shows barriers to RSLs taking on the broader strategic role of sustaining rural communities. Comments ranged from, *"we are not working to a broader strategic agenda"* to *"there are limited opportunities to marry housing and employment"*. Despite these limitations, one RSL described an innovative estate management service using mobile wardens to support elderly people in their tenancies and overcome some deficiencies in rural services and problems of rural isolation. Making the scheme financially viable requires all new tenants to sign up to the service as part of their tenancy agreement, thereby removing tenant choice, though the substantial Housing Plus potential of the scheme was felt to outweigh this issue.

There was also increasing recognition that rural housing enablers are beginning to view rural problems more holistically. In the north-west, one local authority officer argued that the stock transfer process had allowed them to take a step back and operate more strategically. However, RSLs were keen to emphasise that it is not their role, nor do they have the capacity to become directly involved with broader policy issues. A number of associations commented that local authorities should be adopting a stronger enabling role with regard to rural agendas and providing the overarching strategic framework. Some local authority enablers felt that cross-departmental working was emerging around rural strategies and helping to co-ordinate policy responses to problems on the ground. Even so, there was a sense that for some villages such actions have come too late to save the local services. Whilst there was evidence of RSLs becoming more involved in local regeneration and community development work, the urban estates have taken priority so far, with limited development in the rural areas.

CHAPTER 6

CONCLUSIONS

❏ The role and value of social housing for tenants

The first and perhaps most fundamental point to make is the generally very positive views towards their housing of rural RSL tenants interviewed in this study. For the most part, respondents were happy – and in many cases delighted – with their housing and were convinced it met their housing needs more effectively than any housing alternative available in the locality.

In terms of some possible objectives of rural social housing identified in Chapter 1, the most obvious role that the housing fulfilled for tenants was to enable them to remain within established networks of family and friends within a village. The support provided by these networks was often very important to them, and most especially for single parents. Many respondents who had come to the village from elsewhere often stressed the wider benefits of living in a rural location.

Less evidence was found for the possible function of social housing in allowing workers on lower-incomes to live and work within a village. One reason was simply that many tenants were not economically active. There was also a widespread acceptance that the realities of the modern labour markets in rural areas involve extensive commuting, so few people expect to live and work within the same settlement or small locality. The quantitative analysis also cast doubt on any assumption that the availability of affordable housing will, of itself, reduce the migration of young workers in rural areas. Availability of employment opportunities seems to be much the more important issue, and few of the jobs young people get in urban areas will pay well enough for them to be able to commute and so remain within rural areas.

This evidence tends to undermine the rationale most often cited in favour of 'local connection' for rural social housing – to help local people to live and work within the same village. In fact, there were some people in the study areas for whom local connection requirements had actually inhibited employment-related allocations or transfers.

Although the general impact of rural social housing on the lives of tenants was positive, a minority found that living in a village brought with it a sense of isolation, which was only partly due to the lack of access to opportunities and facilities. Social relationships within rural settlements, and the perception by tenants of the attitudes of other residents, led to a minority sensing stigma and hostility. For most tenants, however, relations with other villagers did not seem to be a major issue.

❑ Rural housing providers' concerns and constraints

Rural housing providers' two main worries – shared with their urban counterparts – were the continued residualisation of social housing leading to a future of more transitory and declining demand, and the pressure for greater flexibility in the processes of developing and allocating rural social housing.

Local connections criteria were sometimes seen to be part of a move away from a purely needs-based approach, leading to some RSLs considering themselves to be more forward-looking than the local authority in the area. A less positive assessment of this move away from a needs-based approach is that local connections criteria can, in a formal or informal way, exclude people seen as 'undesirables' by some of a village's residents. The common opposition of the more affluent residents of villages to social housing developments clearly makes RSLs very sensitive to the impact of tenants on the local community, and this may slide under local pressure into exclusionary practices. Local need criteria are clearly a double-edged sword for rural RSLs, and can become one element of the inflexibilities that they see to be a growing problem.

Other problems affecting new social housing development are regional allocations and cost indicators which don't take account of substantial variations in market conditions and costs, even within districts. Housing providers also see local connection criteria, especially where these are written into the initial planning permission, as a major difficulty in then managing the rural housing stock, because they may make it difficult to match a vacancy with a household from a particular settlement. These concerns are all exacerbated for rural social landlords by the small scale of the developments so that, even in a situation of general undersupply of social housing, demand for a specific development in a specific location may disappear.

The Chartered Institute of Housing (1999) argues that there should be opportunities for people with little connection to an area to move into rural areas, and our research reinforces this view. The ability to look to demand beyond the local area is not just an issue for management in making effective use of their stock, but is also a question of meeting the full range of housing needs. The quantitative analysis here emphasised the significance of migration for young people in particular and this challenges a narrow interpretation of local need.

The application of local connection requirements can also be made more flexible by, for example, applying the criteria to a cluster of settlements rather than an individual village. Flexibility could also be applied to policies on transfers and exchanges within the social rented sector: one RSL raised the possibility of a partnership approach to transfers, given that that their own stock was scattered over a broad geographical area and limited in number in any one location.

Housing providers were certainly aware of issues of polarisation, and allocation systems based on local needs, and the desire to 'manage' the profile of their tenants, could lead to a more varied and less stigmatised 'community housing' sector. The involvement of rural RSLs in a more comprehensive Housing Plus agenda to actively address wider issues of disadvantage and exclusion is more uncertain. Though practices such as door-to-door rent collection do allow close contact with tenants, a 'hands-off' style of management seemed to be the general preference of tenants. Enthusiasm for tenant participation in particular seemed very limited on the part of both landlords and tenants. As for the more general issues of isolation and lack of access to facilities, plus similar types of rural areas, RSLs appeared to favour working in partnership with other agencies to provide a wider range of services to their tenants.

❏ Variations between rural housing markets

As a cornerstone of both the quantitative analyses and the interview-based qualitative case studies, the new classification of rural housing markets has proved its value. The variety in rural housing market conditions is an essential part of a real understanding of the links between housing and local social and economic circumstances. The classification's ward-level detail highlighted the variation existing over short distances, a finding borne out in the case study research which often found strong differences within the same district. Even so, the classification did not always reveal simple, clear-cut distinctions between the experiences of people in different types of area.

For example, the problem of affordability in the market sector was a theme common to the experience of social housing tenants in case study areas – both north and south – with most tenants seeing the bottom rung of the ladder of owner occupation to be well out of reach. Paradoxically, social landlords throughout the case studies worried about possible loss of demand for parts of the rural housing stock, although in some areas this concern might be limited to specific dwelling-types or developments, especially one-bedroom sheltered accommodation.

The national analyses sought to tease out the extent to which living in a village with a reasonable level of social housing provision benefits not just the tenants but the village's residents more generally. A particularly notable finding was that these class 1 villages had seen their young people move away rapidly during the 1980s. It seems likely that the most important issue for young people is the limited job opportunities in the countryside, and the fact that accessible employment has declined in class 1 villages thus outweighs these areas' better housing opportunities in producing the strong movement away of young people. This interpretation is reinforced by the fact that it is the rural areas with the least local housing opportunities, but the most buoyant local economies, where young people are most likely to stay. In a similar vein, the higher level of poverty in the class 1 areas produces village-wide problems that the availability of social housing cannot offset.

These analyses could be seen to suggest that the presence of social housing in villages makes a relatively modest difference to the 'life chances' of those villages' residents. Even so, the constantly increasing pressure to house more of England's escalating number of households is fuelling shortages of the affordable housing necessary to sustain socially-balanced communities. Thus the provision of more affordable housing of good quality for low-income residents – in a situation where this will not be done by any other part of the local housing system – is the most important contribution that RSLs can make. Given that the difficulties RSLs face in providing new social housing in rural areas can be out of all proportion to the small number of dwellings involved, RSLs deserve every encouragement to redouble their efforts to reduce the current unmet needs for affordable rural housing.

REFERENCES

Bibby P and Shepherd J (1997) *The Housing Corporation and the Rural Development Commission's rural settlement gazetteer* (Research Source 26). London: Housing Corporation.

Bramley G (1990) *Bridging the affordability gap in 1990*. London: Association of District Councils and Housing Federation.

Bramley G and Smart G (1995) *Rural incomes and housing affordability*. Salisbury: Rural Development Commission.

Burrows R and Rhodes D (1998) *Unpopular places? Area disadvantage and the geography of misery in England*. Bristol: Policy Press.

Cartmel F and Furlong A (2000) *Youth unemployment in rural areas*. York: York Publishing Services.

Chaplin R, Martin S, Royce C, Saw P, Whitehead C and Yang, J. (1995) *Housing Associations, Private Finance and Market Rents in England's Rural Districts*. Cambridge: Department of Land Economy, University of Cambridge.

Chapman P, Phiminster E, Schucksmith M, Upward R, and Vera-Toscana E (1998) *Poverty and exclusion in rural Britain: the dynamics of local income and employment*. York: York Publishing Services.

Chartered Institute of Housing (1999) *Response to DETR/MAFF discussion paper: Rural England*. Coventry: CIH.

Cloke P, Milbourne P and Thomas C (1994) *Lifestyles in rural England* (Research Report 18). London: Rural Development Commission.

Constable M (1999) "Rural housing needs help" *Local Council Review*, July, pp12-13.

Coombes M and Raybould S (2000) "Policy-relevant surfaced data on population distribution and characteristics" *Transactions in GIS* 4: forthcoming.

Countryside Agency, The (1999) *The state of the countryside 1999*. Cheltenham: The Countryside Agency.

Craig J (1987) "An urban-rural categorisation of wards and local authorities" *Population Trends* 47: 6-11.

Denham C and White I (1998) "Differences in urban and rural Britain" *Population Trends* 91: 23-34.

Department of Environment (1993) *Population distribution; deprivation of settlement pattern indicators* (Settlement Working Group paper SSASG (93) 95). London: Department of Environment.

Department of Environment, Transport and the Regions, Ministry of Agriculture, Fisheries and Food (1999) *Rural England: A Discussion Document*. London: DETR and MAFF.

Department of Environment, Transport and the Regions (1999) *Housing In England 1997/98* (Housing Statistics Summaries 2) http://www.housing.detr.gov.uk/research/hss/002/index.htm

Department of Environment, Transport and the Regions (2000) *PPG 3: Housing*. London: DETR.

DTZ Pieda Consulting (1998) *The nature of demand for housing in rural areas*. London: DETR.

Forrest R and Murie A (1992) *Housing change in a rural area: an analysis of dwelling histories*. Working paper 101. Bristol: School for Advanced Urban Studies.

Illouz-Winicki C and Paillard D (1998) "New business in rural areas" *The OECD Observer* 210: 12-16.

Joseph Rowntree Foundation (1999) *Response to discussion document on rural England*. York: Joseph Rowntree Foundation.

Jupp B (2000) *Living together: community life on mixed tenure estates*. London: Demos.

Lee P and Murie A (1997) *Poverty, housing tenure and social exclusion*. Bristol: Policy Press.

Marsh A and Mullins D (1998) *Housing, and public policy: citizenship, choice and control*. Buckingham: Open University Press.

Mullins D (1993) *An evaluation of the Housing Corporation Rural Programme*. Salisbury: Rural Development Commission.

Oldfield King Planning Ltd. (1997) *Housing Plus in Rural Areas*. London: Housing Corporation, Rural Development Corporation, Hastoe Housing Association, Devon and Cornwall Housing Association.

Performance and Innovation Unit (Cabinet Office) (1999) *Rural economies*. http://www.cabinet-office.gov.uk/innovation/1999/rural/index.htm

Phillips D and Williams AM (1982) *Rural housing and the public sector*. Aldershot: Gower.

Power A and Mumford K (1999) *The slow death of great cities: urban abandonment or urban renaissance?* York: YPS.

Richardson K and Curbishley P (1999) *Frequent movers: looking for love?* York: Joseph Rowntree Foundation.

Rugg J and Jones A (1999) *Getting a job, finding a home: rural youth transitions*. Bristol: Policy Press.

Shucksmith M (1981) *No homes for locals?* Farnborough: Gower.

Shucksmith M, Henderson M, Raybould S, Coombes M and Wong C (1995) *A classification of rural housing markets in England*. London: HMSO.

Shucksmith M, Roberts D, Scott D, Chapman P and Conway E (1996) *Disadvantage in rural areas*. Salisbury: Rural Development Commission.

Simmons M (1997) *Landscapes of Poverty: Aspects of Rural England in the late 1990s*. London: Lemos and Crane.

Social Exclusion Unit (1999) *Report of Action Team on unpopular housing*. London: Stationery Office.

Wong C and Madden M (2000) *North West regional housing need and demand research*. London: DETR.

Figure 1: Rural England

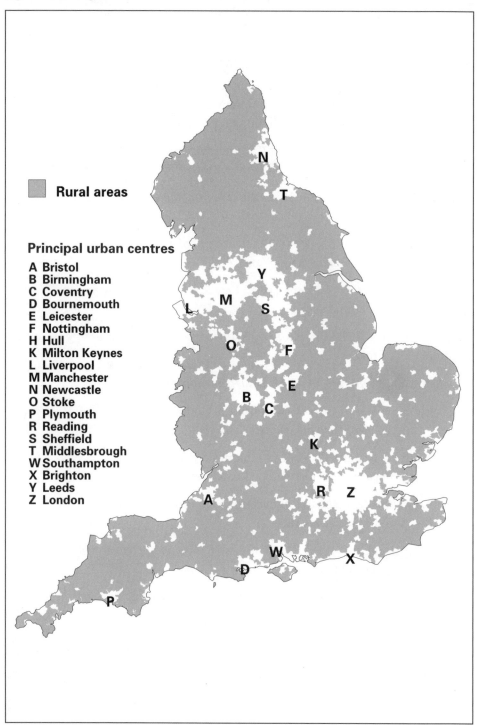

Rural areas

Principal urban centres
A Bristol
B Birmingham
C Coventry
D Bournemouth
E Leicester
F Nottingham
H Hull
K Milton Keynes
L Liverpool
M Manchester
N Newcastle
O Stoke
P Plymouth
R Reading
S Sheffield
T Middlesbrough
W Southampton
X Brighton
Y Leeds
Z London

Figure 2: Accessibility of rural areas

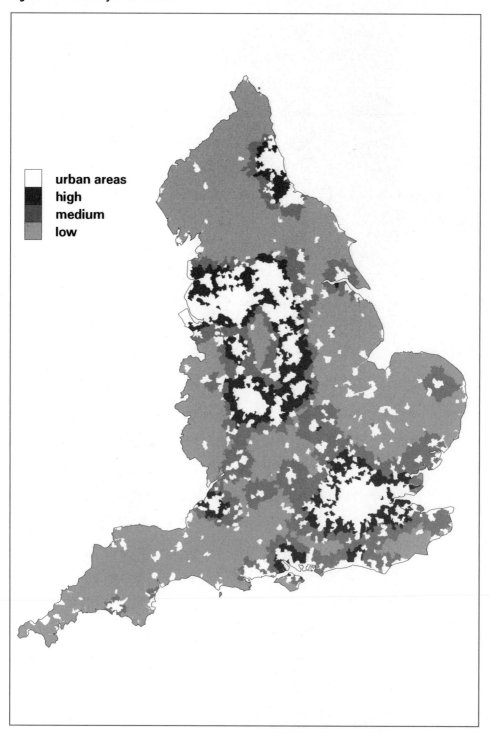

urban areas
high
medium

Figure 3: Rural areas with substantial levels of social housing in 1981

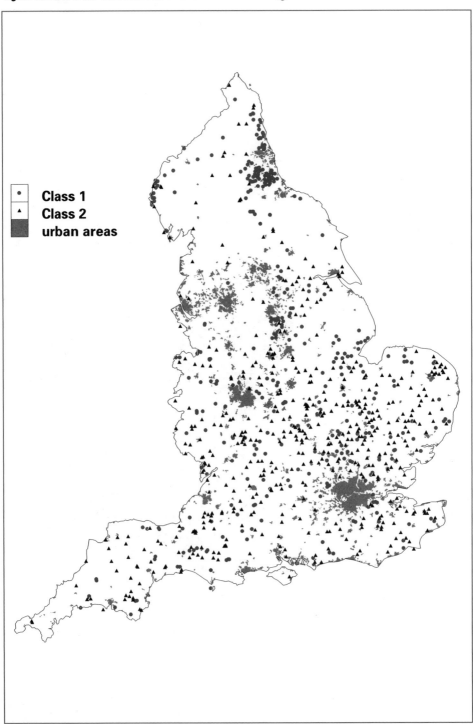

Figure 4: Other rural areas – substantial levels of out-commuting

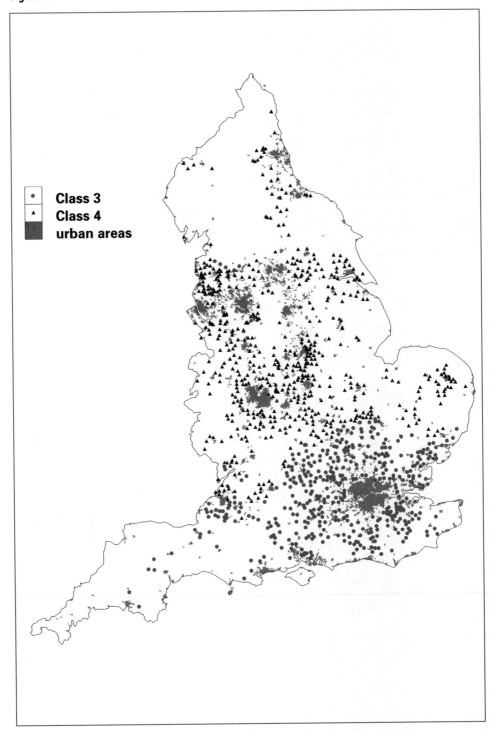

Class 3
Class 4
urban areas

Figure 5: Other rural areas – lower levels of out-commuting

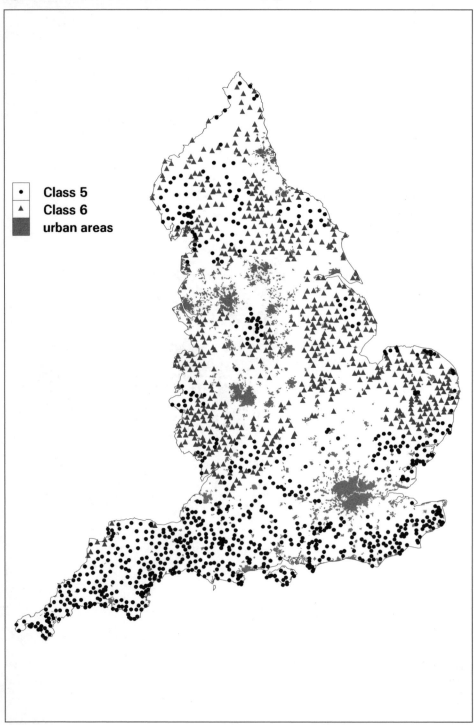

- • Class 5
- ▲ Class 6
- ■ urban areas

Appendix 1

Proposals for Affordable Housing in the Rural White Paper

This Appendix provides a summary of the commitments to action made by DETR in the Rural White Paper to increase the supply of affordable housing in Rural England.

■ Overall summary of measures

- Doubling funding for the Housing Corporation between 2000 and 2003 to benefit both rural and urban areas.

- Doubling the size of the Housing Corporation's programme in small rural settlements from 800 to 1,600 homes a year.

- Local authorities able to charge the full council tax on second homes and retain extra revenue (subject to consultation).

- Better use of the planning system to secure more affordable homes as part of mixed developments in market towns and rural areas. There is no reason why, in small villages if there is evidence of need and subject to financial viability, every new market house should not be matched with an affordable home.

- Better designed homes to fit in with rural surroundings.

- Package of VAT reforms to encourage additional conversions of properties for residential use.

■ Detailed measures

- Provide practical examples of where rural authorities are planning successfully for affordable housing.

- Encourage local authorities to consider whether the Local Authority Social Housing Grant could be used to ensure that the potential of exceptions sites is used to the full.

- The Countryside Agency will continue to fund its successful Rural Housing Enabler programme and explore extending it to more rural areas. Remind authorities in rural areas where there is a significant demand for affordable housing to consider the possibility of applying for designation.

- Proposal (subject to consultation) to give local authorities discretion to charge the full council tax on second homes, rather than the 50 per cent discount that they are required to apply at the moment. The extra revenue raised should be retained by the local authorities concerned and funds may be earmarked to provide affordable homes in the areas affected.

- Fairer Right to Buy discounts introduced in 1999, replacing the cash limit of £50,000 by new regional cash limits ranging from £22,000 to £38,000 meaning that the most expensive properties in attractive high demand rural areas will be sold only at a fair price.

- Promote more flexible lettings policies by local authorities, so as to take more account of specific rural needs in their area. Over the next three years, £11m provided to support pilot schemes involving local authorities and registered social landlords which test choice-based lettings policies. Intend to invite pilots from rural areas.

- Funding the Empty Homes Agency to work with local authorities to bring more empty rural property back into use.

- Ask the Regional Development Agencies and the Countryside Agency to address the issue of empty properties and promote the actions required to bring more of them back into productive use as part of the economic regeneration of rural areas.

- As announced in the November 2000 Pre-Budget Report, plan to encourage additional conversion of properties for residential use by cutting the VAT rate to 5 per cent for residential conversions and removing the VAT burden on the sale of renovated houses that have been empty for ten years or more.

- Increase the level of support to help those on modest incomes acquire their own homes. Options include part buying and part renting homes from registered social landlords (RSLs) or using an interest free equity loan from an RSL toward the cost of a property e.g. Homebuy.

- Starter Home Initiative will assist key workers with home ownership in areas of high prices and high demand. The Spending Review has provided £250m to support this important initiative and will be available to benefit rural high demand hotspots, among other areas.

APPENDIX 2

CONTRASTING DEFINITIONS OF INDIVIDUAL RURAL AREAS

	Rural areas in this classification	Areas in the Rural Settlement Gazetteer
'Building block' areas	1991 wards	1991 Enumeration Districts (EDs)
	EDs are substantially more detailed than wards	
Areas excluded as urban	Wards whose populations primarily live in urban settlements of over 10,000 people.	All EDs falling within urban areas of over 10,000 people.
	Urban settlements as defined by DoE (1993) were in places subdivided into Urban Areas according to pre-1974 local authority boundaries (for example, the part of the W. Yorkshire conurbation which used to be Heckmondwike MB is deemed a separate Urban Area and – as its population is less than 10,000 – it is in fact included in the Rural Settlement Gazetteer whereas it is excluded from this classification).	
Areas identified as small towns	Wards, or groups thereof, approximating to urban settlements of under 10,000.	Groups of EDs falling within urban areas of under 10,000 people.
Other rural areas	Individual wards whose populations mostly live outside any single urban settlement (n.b. a very small minority of wards in metropolitan counties have very large populations, but emerge here as 'rural' because no single urban settlement includes half their residents).	EDs, or groups thereof, approximating to the sets of postcodes which share the same 'locality' name – as the line above the post town – in their official post office addresses (n.b. around 50 villages appear to be included *both* in this category *and* among the small towns).

(Source: Bibby and Shepherd, 1997)

APPENDIX 3

CREATING THE CLASSIFICATION

Variables included in the Axes

Axis 1	Rate of planning application refusals
	Rate of new house building
	Average house price
	Area in national park or Area of Outstanding National Beauty
Axis 2	Proportion of houses sold for £39,000 or less
	Urbanisation Index
	Household to dwelling ratio
	Proportion of concealed households
	Proportion of in-movers that are retired
	Proportion of housing that are holiday homes
	Proportion of housing that second homes
	Household headship rate
	Proportion of household heads aged under 30
	Residential turnover
	Unemployment rate
	Owner occupancy rate in lower middle income groups
	Economic activity rate of married women
	Proportion of workers commuting under 5 km
	Proportion of workers commuting over 20 kms
Axis 3	Social housing as share of 1991 housing stock
	Change in social housing's share 1981-1991

■ Definition of the rural area classes

Taking account of their relative importance to this study, it was decided to build the classification by giving the highest priority to axis 3, then 2 and the lowest to axis 1. The primary criteria used were measures of the level of social housing provision in 1991 and the change in that level over the preceding decade. In producing the classification, the analyses were carried out in such a way as to ensure that a very similar proportion of England's rural population fell into each class.

Axis 3: Was the social housing share of 1991 housing stock over 20%?				
Yes	No			
	Was the social housing share in 1981 over 20% but declining 1981-1991 by over 7.5%?			
	Yes	No		
Class 1	Class 2	Class 3	Class 5	**Axis 1:** Higher supply constraints
		Class 4	Class 6	Lower supply constraints
		Out-commuters **Axis 2:** Key element of incomer housing demand	Holiday-makers and people retiring	

■ Overcoming technical obstacles

The figure below illustrates the complexity, which has to be handled in order to cope with data inputs from various sources at several points in time. It can be seen that Geographic Information System (GIS) techniques are essential for bringing the data onto a common set of areas. For example, a house price dataset was available for individual properties, with each house's location identified by postcode sector (such as: NE11 7). Postcode sectors are too small for entirely reliable averages to be produced at this level, and they cannot be grouped in a way which matches the boundaries of the 1991 wards which are the units of analysis here. The solution is to use a GIS technique which estimates a 'surface', to show the accessibility of rural areas (Coombes and Raybould, 2000), by producing an average, for each ward in turn, drawing on the evidence of all house prices in postcode sectors within quite a wide area around that ward's central point. This average places progressively less weight on evidence from areas which are further away. The result is a 'surface' of values which are different for each ward, but which smoothes out more extreme variations between adjacent wards (such variations being more likely to be due to the small number of houses sold in some individual postcode sectors, rather than to genuine strong contrasts in prices between adjacent areas). This analysis – applied to every rural ward in turn, taking account of jobs and population in both urban and rural areas nearby – produces a surface declining relatively smoothly away from its main peak in central London and the subsidiary peaks in other major cities. This provides a set of values approximating the pressure for development from the main urban areas.

Producing the 1991-based housing market classification

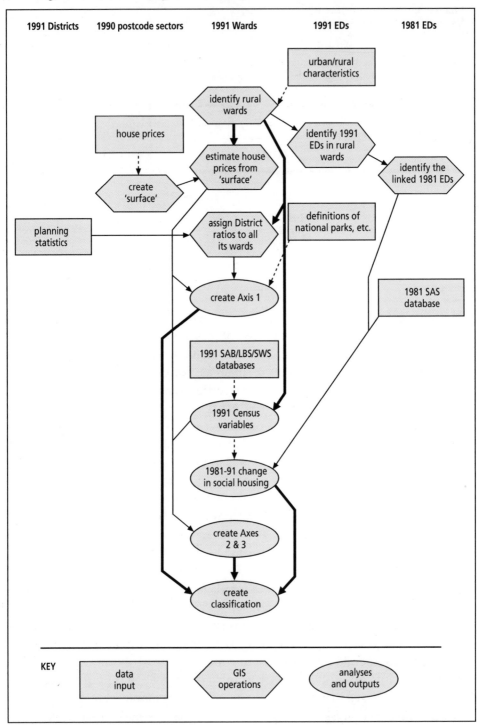

Appendix 4

Districts Used as Case Studies: Key Characteristics and Case Study Details

Rural housing market Class the District typifies	Region in which the District is located	Number of RSL dwellings in any part of the District	Per cent of District's 1991 households living in social housing	Designated areas in the District	Average weekly rent for a 2 bedroom RSL dwelling	Rural enabler(s) interviewed	RSLs studied: scale of operation; specialism if any	Number of rural schemes studied [number of rented dwellings]	Were the schemes under S106?
1	North-west	4,833	26%	partly in a national park	£45.50 – £50.50	independent organisation & local authority	RSL1: county; general RSL2: national; general	9 [55] 3 [15]	mix yes
2	East midlands	329	15%	none	£58.00	none	RSL3: county; specialist rural RSL4: regional; general	4 [34] 1 [11]	mix mix
3	South-east	6,006	14%	partly in an Area of Outstanding Natural Beauty	£56.00 – £65.00	rural housing trust	RSL5: county; general RSL6: region; general RSL7: national; general RSL8: district; general	3 [21] 6 [64] 1 [6] n/a	mix mix mix n/a
5	South-west	825	15%	none	£49.00	rural housing trust	RSL9: regional; general RSL10: county; specialist rural	4 [46] 4 [21]	no mix
4 & 6 (mix)	Yorkshire and the Humber	1,661	13%	partly in an Area of Outstanding Natural Beauty	£52.30	rural housing trust & local authority officer	RSL11: regional; general RSL12: national; specialist elderly RSL13: national; general RSL14: national; general	2 [14] 3 [33] 1 [6] n/a	mix mix mix n/a

APPENDIX 5

THE LONGITUDINAL ANALYSIS

One of the difficulties in this analysis has been disentangling influences at the area-level from those factors relating to individuals or households. One class of area may have a higher level of social housing provision than most others, but how have any observable differences between this class of area and the other classes actually come about? It might be that people in social housing tend to experience a particular outcome wherever they live, so the difference for a class of areas is simply due to the compositional effect of that area's population. On the other hand, genuine area effects might occur where everyone locally is affected to some degree by the availability of social housing in the village. The only way to disentangle these genuinely area-level effects from the compositional effects, is to analyse data on individuals so that such influences as 'being a social housing tenant', and 'being in an area where there are large numbers of social housing tenants', can be separately taken into account.

The datasets analysed here are the Longitudinal Study (LS), covering the 1981-1991 period, and the British Household Panel Survey (BHPS) for the 1991-1998 period. Neither dataset is available for both periods, so to provide a comparison of the 1980s with the 1990s it is necessary to 'work around' the differences between the two, which are summarised below. These datasets are here explored using Logit analyses, also described below.

■ Analyses of the longitudinal datasets

The key challenge for these analyses is to disentangle the influence of a person's own characteristics from the influence, if any, of the area in which they live. Does living in any of the six rural area classes improve various 'life chances' or not? A central question here is whether the 'average' resident of a class 1 area (who may or may not themselves live in social housing), tends to benefit from living in an area where there is still a reasonable level of social housing. The way to disentangle such *contextual* effects is to carry out Logit analyses, using datasets which separately identify as many as possible of the relevant individual and household characteristics of the sample population.

Key features of the LS and BHPS datasets

	Longitudinal Study	British Household Panel Survey
Origins of information	Confidential individual and household data from Census and statutory registration systems (births, deaths and notifiable diseases) since 1971.	Annual survey of individuals in selected households, beginning in 1991.
Linkage and attrition	Mainly manual tracing by birth date and name; official data misses few people so attrition rate is low.	Linkage is automatic once response received; academic surveys receive lower response rates so attrition is notable.
Sampling procedure	All individuals born on any of 4 pre-selected dates in the year comprise the sample.	Random sample of households within geographically stratified postcode sectors.
Population covered	All ages are included in the LS but these analyses only cover those aged 12-74 in 1981.	All aged over 16 are included in the BHPS but these analyses cover those aged 16-74 in 1991.
Cases excluded	Anyone not living in England in both 1981 and 1991.	Anyone not living in England in both 1991 and 1997.
Cases analysed	300,683	6,464

For each type of variable – such as age groups, or types of area – a reference group is identified prior to the analysis and then the Logit results report the way in which the experience of people in the other groups of that type differs from the experience of those in the reference group.

The first issue for any analysis here will be whether the experience of people in rural areas in general can be seen to be measurably different from that of urban area residents. As a result, urban areas provide the most appropriate reference group to compare each of these rural area classes against. This strategy would ordinarily create a problem due to both the LS and BHPS – as befits their role as representative national samples – containing far more people in urban rather than rural areas. The problem would be that any distinctive relationship between two variables in rural, as against urban, areas would tend to be 'swamped' in the analysis by the experience of the far more numerous urban members of the sample. These analyses avoid this problem by substantially 'down-weighting' the urban cases so that, in effect, they have a similar influence on the overall results as do any one of the six rural area classes. In this way, people in urban areas remain the *reference group* which each rural area class can be compared against, but the relationships between other variables (e.g. social class and tenure) are predominantly measured by reference to the experience of people in rural areas.

The results from the Logit analyses are reported in the form of odds ratios: these represent the likelihood of that group of people experiencing the outcome of interest, with this likelihood expressed relative to the equivalent likelihood of the reference group for that variable. Thus a value of 1.33 for group X can be interpreted as, *"people in group X were around a third as likely again as those in the reference group"* to have experienced the outcome of interest. In the same way, a value of .66 means that the likelihood for the group was only about two-thirds of that of the reference group. If the odds ratio is shown in a Table without an accompanying asterisk then the difference between the group's likelihood and that of the reference group is not statistically significant.